W9-AHS-198

# JIM GEORGE

# *The* Man
# Who Makes a
# Difference

HARVEST HOUSE PUBLISHERS

EUGENE, OREGON

Unless otherwise indicated, all Scripture quotations are taken from the Holy Bible: New International Version®. NIV®. Copyright © 1973, 1978, 1984 by the International Bible Society. Used by permission of Zondervan Publishing House. The "NIV" and "New International Version" trademarks are registered in the United States Patent and Trademark Office by International Bible Society.

Verses marked NASB are taken from the New American Standard Bible®, © 1960, 1962, 1963, 1968, 1971, 1972, 1973, 1975, 1977, 1995 by The Lockman Foundation. Used by permission.

Verses marked NKJV are taken from the New King James Version. Copyright © 1982 by Thomas Nelson, Inc. Used by permission. All rights reserved.

Verses marked KJV are taken from the King James Version of the Bible.

*Italicized words in Scripture quotes indicate emphasis added by the author.*

*Cover by Dugan Design Group, Bloomington, Minnesota*

*Cover photo © iStockphoto / photoblanko40*

**THE MAN WHO MAKES A DIFFERENCE**
Copyright © 2003/2010 by Jim George
Published by Harvest House Publishers
Eugene, Oregon 97402
www.harvesthousepublishers.com

Library of Congress Cataloging-in-Publication Data

George, Jim
The man who makes a difference / Jim George.
    p. cm.
Rev. ed. of: God's man of influence.
Includes bibliographical references (p. ).
ISBN 978-0-7369-2071-1 (pbk.)
1. Christian men—Religious life. 2. Influence (Psychology)—Religious aspects—Christianity. I. George, Jim, 1943- God's man of influence. II. Title.
BV4528.2.G455 2010

248.8'42—dc22

2010011606

**All rights reserved.** No part of this publication may be reproduced, stored in a retrieval system, or transmitted in any form or by any means—electronic, mechanical, digital, photocopy, recording, or any other—except for brief quotations in printed reviews, without the prior permission of the publisher.

Printed in the United States of America

11  12  13  14  15  16  17  18  / BP-NI /  10  9  8  7  6  5  4  3  2

# CONTENTS

## Ten Keys to a Life of Impact

### Key #1—The Bible

### Key #2—Prayer

### Key #3—Obedience

### Key #4—Challenges

### Key #5—Discipline

# A Word of Welcome

What does a man who makes a difference look like and what does he do? What makes his life a life of lasting impact?

For the past 30 years, I have sought to become that kind of man. I have studied the character of the men of influence God has placed in my life. I have also searched the Scriptures to glean an understanding of the traits of the godly men of the Bible.

What a joy it has been these past years to immerse myself in the study of men who have made a difference to their family, church, community, and world—more specifically, the kind of influence that makes a lasting impact. For instance,

> Influence is a process.
>
> Influence is costly.
>
> Influence is never neutral.
>
> Influence is powerful.
>
> Influence is about people.

Influence is demanding.

Influence is hard won.

Influence is easily lost.

Influence is to be desired.

Influence is everyone's privilege.

Influence is everyone's responsibility.

Influence is affected by relationships.

Influence is attainable by anyone.

I am especially glad that you, too, desire to become a man who makes a difference—a man who has a lasting impact. And I look forward to our journey together toward becoming men who make a difference. Join with me as we take a journey of discovery through the lives of a handful of history's greatest men of influence from the Bible. We'll look in particular at the life of the apostle Paul, who has long been of special interest to me. And there are a few others who I have been privileged to meet along my own journey. Join with me as we discover ten keys of growth and maturity that will prepare you to have a dynamic life of impact. And, if you want to journey with me a little further, you will enjoy going through the application questions at the back of this book.

May God encourage and strengthen you as you make the journey of your life—the journey of becoming a man who makes a difference.

Your fellow traveler,
Jim George

*My life shall touch a dozen lives*
*before this day is done,*
*Leave countless marks for good or ill*
*ere sets the evening sun.*
*This is the wish I always wish,*
*the prayer I always pray:*
*Lord, may my life help other lives*
*it touches by the way.*[1]

# Profiling the Man
# Who Makes a Difference

*With God all things are possible.*
—Matthew 19:26

❧

In his 1955 Pulitzer Prize-winning book *Profiles in Courage,* the late president of the United States John F. Kennedy chronicled the life and stories of eight U.S. senators. He described and outlined how these men endured the pressures of public office—the risks to their careers, popularity with the people, defamation of their characters—all with great courage.

That book had a great impact on many in the 1960s generation and beyond. Kennedy was not only a president, he was also an historian—he researched the elements that demonstrated the courage of these political figures.[2] His book gave readers a better understanding of the lives and struggles of these eight senators.

I understand that the word *profiling* is not politically correct, and that profiling can be abused and cause great harm. But despite its "bad press," profiling can be a beneficial exercise for us as we set out on our journey to understand some of the characteristics or keys to a life of impact. In my dictionary, *profiling* is defined as developing a list of characteristics that represent someone or something. This means that others can look at another person's life and develop a list of characteristics, such as his or her habits, principles, beliefs, and views. This list would then represent that person's life, becoming his or her profile.

## The Profile of Your Life

Every person has a profile. Each person's profile—his or her patterns, habits, principles, and beliefs—indicates who he or she is as an individual. For instance, as a jogger, I have a specific profile. If you were to look at my life as a jogger you would see that I fit into a certain category of athletic endeavor and health. My professional status of pastor, writer, speaker, and teacher also gives me a certain profile. In fact, every profession and area of work has a specific profile.

Have you ever thought about your personal profile and whether your life will have a lasting impact? If people took a long look at your life, what would they see? Then, if they published their "research," what characteristics would they report by the patterns of your life? What qualities and habits would be evident for all to witness? In what ways are you impacting the lives of others?

I confess I'm not always pleased with the profile of my life! And the same is probably true of how you feel about your habits and activities, too. This is because, no matter what our profile, there is always room to grow. But one of the best ways for us to evaluate our own level of impact and possibly make some changes (hopefully for the better) is to look at the profiles of others whose lives are worthy of copying.

So, together, let's think about our own life while we look to the lives of others. See what we can learn about becoming a man who makes a difference.

## The Qualities of a Man Who Makes a Difference

Let's begin our list of qualities or keys by looking at the life of the apostle Paul. Let's spend some time profiling the characteristics of this man's amazing life. Why Paul? Because Paul lived...

- a life of obedience to the Lord's commands
- a life of service to others
- a life of meekness and humility
- a life of prayer
- a life full of faith and trust
- a life of empowerment by the Spirit
- a life of loving and studying the Scriptures
- a life of modeling Christlikeness for others to follow
- a life of faithfulness to the end

Wouldn't you like to have this kind of a profile? I know I would! And God has given us Paul as a prime example to follow. What Christian man wouldn't want to live as powerfully as Paul did? By modeling our lives after this amazing man, you and I can have a greater impact on our home, family, workplace, church, and neighborhood! As we look at how God worked through Paul (and others), let's determine together, from the start, to let God work in us and make some key changes in our lives.

This is my prayer for you and me:

that we would exhibit an open heart as we move through our profiling journey,

that we would be sensitive to the Lord's prompting as we examine the powerful life of Paul and others,

that we would be willing to make drastic changes if the Lord so directs, and that we prayerfully ask God for a greater passion for living the Christian life.

Are you up for the challenge, my friend? I'm trusting that you are!

## The Profile of a Man Who Makes a Difference

*Paul.* Just say the name and a myriad of faces come to mind. For me, the name *Paul* reminds me of my two sons-in-law, both named Paul. For you, Paul may have been the name of an old buddy from days gone by. But as we begin our profiling journey, the Paul we are thinking about is the apostle Paul. Why Paul? What was so unique about his life that would make him worthy of our attention as a man of influence?

On the surface, Paul the apostle wasn't much of a physical specimen. One writer pictured him as "half-bald" and "bandy-legged."[3] A second-century church leader described Paul as "a man small of stature, with a bald head and crooked legs...with eyebrows meeting and nose somewhat hooked."[4] Well, friend, neither of these descriptions portrays Paul as a man of which legends are made.

No, it wasn't a commanding physical presence that made Paul such an outstanding Christian personality. It was his powerful life. And that's what we want to profile. Paul's life was characterized by love, compassion, peace, humility, focus, and numerous other noble qualities that made him a powerful force for the Christian faith, that made him a man of influence.

It's been said the apostle Paul was the most outstanding personality the Christian faith has ever produced.[5] That is an incredible statement to make about just one man out of the millions who have named the name of Christ as their Savior. Recently I re-read a book about Paul entitled *The Man Who Shook the World.*[6] This amazing title is used to describe the life of just one man among the myriads of believers who have lived down through the centuries of Christendom. Clearly, Paul had a significant impact on the world around him.

As you and I profile the influential life of the apostle Paul through the lens of Scripture, we can't help but notice these accomplishments and more:

- *Paul wrote 13 God-inspired books of the New Testament.* The apostle John wrote five books, and the great apostle Peter wrote only two. (Paul's feat seems more amazing when we consider that in his day, writing was done on animal skins and pressed reeds with quilled feathers, using a mixture of charcoal and water for ink. Why, Paul didn't even have "spell check"!)

- *Paul's writings documented many of the essential doctrinal truths of the Christian faith.* God communicated many foundational truths of Christianity through Paul, and the church has been able to build and grow on those truths over the last 1900 years (truths about justification by faith, the church as the body of Christ, spiritual gifts, the deity of Christ, the resurrection, the return of Christ, and the kingdom of God, just to name a few).

- *Paul was a pioneer missionary and church planter.* Missionaries and church planters have spent the last 19 centuries patterning their strategies after Paul's effective and fruitful life and model. (As a former missionary, I have read numerous books that detail Paul's missionary journeys and their applications for today.)

- *Paul was one of the great disciplers of men.* He raised up countless godly men to continue his work of ministry. Today we are still being challenged to fulfill the pattern set forth by Paul's admonition to one of his disciples— "The things you have heard me say in the presence of many witnesses entrust to reliable men who will also be qualified to teach others" (2 Timothy 2:2). (I have spent most of my adult Christian life following the pattern set by Paul in this verse—first, in my own training by "reliable men," and then by passing on that training to "others.")

## The Path to Becoming a Man Who Makes a Difference

However, there is a side of Paul and his life of impact that almost no one talks about: Paul's life was filled with *adversity*. He was constantly misunderstood by his fellow believers. He was relentlessly harassed by the enemies of the gospel. He spent many days, weeks, months, and even years in jails because of his faith. There are also a handful of additional facts about Paul's life and service to Christ that could be seen as "strikes" against him. If you or I ever think God cannot use us in mighty ways because of the adversities we have encountered, think again! If you ever get discouraged because of what seem to be "strikes" against you, think again! Remember the following facts about the path of Paul's life:

- *Paul did not become a Christian until he was more than 30 years old.* The majority of people who become Christians come to Christ before the age of 15.

- *Paul did not start his formal ministry until he was over 40.* Most pastoral search committees would never consider the résumé of a man over 40 with little or no ministry experience! They are looking for a 40-year-old pastor with 15 to 20 years of pastoral experience. This standard would have caused a search committee to pass over the great and powerful apostle Paul as a candidate for ministry.

- *Paul did not make his first missionary journey until he was over 45.* Many churches today send missionaries to the field right after they graduate from Bible school in their early twenties. Seldom do we send a middle-aged man to the mission field. We erroneously wonder, *What could he do? He's too old!* and fail to ask, "Who do you think is probably more mature—a man in his early twenties or a man in his early forties?"

- *Paul did not write his first book of the Bible until he was 49 years old.* This was 15 years after his conversion. Those

15 years gave Paul time to mature in his faith and time to have something to say. And, speaking of adversity, many of Paul's letters were written while he was a prisoner, chained to a Roman soldier!

- *Paul did not shun hardship and persecution.* His missionary travels of thousands of miles were mostly on foot or in crude, first-century sailing vessels. He also admits to frequent floggings, exposure to death, multiple imprisonments, five times receiving 39 lashes, beatings, and stonings…not to mention shipwrecks and the lack of a permanent home (2 Corinthians 11:23-27). By the time most Christians reach their forties, they can't walk two miles, are already looking forward to retirement, and would define *hardship* as waiting 30 minutes to be seated at their favorite restaurant.

In spite of getting a late start in the Christian life and the physical hardships he endured, Paul had a great impact. Paul's influence *began* when most men are beginning to pull out of the fast lane. What a challenge this should be to those of us who are getting on in age…say, 40! Two lessons from Paul shout across the centuries to you and me—*it's never too late to serve God, and it's never too late to change the course of your life so that you can make a difference.* No matter how difficult your circumstances, God can still use you to serve Him and others.

## The Pattern of Your Life

I trust this brief profile of Paul of Tarsus encourages you. (I know it encourages me!) Whatever your age or your situation, or whatever adversities you are experiencing or number of strikes against you, with God's help, the best of your life and your greatest impact is yet to come. God shows us in the life of Paul that adversity is the seedbed of achievement. Hardship is often the training ground for a life of impact.

Are you beginning to see why Paul's life and ministry are so unique and compelling? Already we find ourselves challenged by this man's life, and we've just started! I'm sure you are as curious as I am as to what made this man tick. Well, take courage. We'll get there. We'll find the answers, and we'll find out what made other great men of influence tick as well.

But first…a word about you. If people were to profile and chronicle the pattern of your life, what would they see? Are there any contradictions? Are there any inconsistencies, any "blips on the screen"? Are there some "strikes" against you on your record? Is there a long list of suffering and adversity? Or does your date of birth reveal that time is running out, that not too many years are left, that perhaps you're a late bloomer?

If you're like me, the pattern of your life probably looks a little rocky. But be encouraged! You (and I) are in good company—the company of the apostle Paul. With God, all things are possible (Matthew 19:26). *He* is able to transform you into a man of influence, into a man whose life has a lasting impact on others and on the world if you are willing to make some sacrifices. What are the sacrifices you will need to make? You must be willing to make some changes in your own life. If you want to see a change in others, you must begin with yourself. We see this affirmed in the following words, which appear on the tomb of an Anglican bishop at Westminster Abbey:

> When I was young and free, my imagination had no limits. I dreamed of changing the world. But as I grew older and wiser, I discovered that the world would not change. So I shortened my sights somewhat and I decided on changing my country. But it too seemed immoveable. Then as I grew into my twilight years, in one last desperate attempt, I settled for changing only my family, those closest to me. But alas, they would have not of it. And now as I lie on my death bed, I suddenly realize. If only I had changed myself first, then by example I would have changed my family. From their inspiration and encouragement, I then would be able to better my country, and who knows, I may have even changed my world.[7]

*He is no fool who gives what he cannot keep*
*to gain what he cannot lose.*[1]
—Jim Elliot

# Taking the First Step

*If anyone is in Christ, he is a new creation;*
*the old has gone, the new has come!*
—2 Corinthians 5:17

L ife is full of surprises…and usually we're not prepared for them. You and I never know when we get out of bed each morning what events during the day might end up having a marked effect on us, do we? And when surprises do hit us, we usually end up asking, "What happened?"

When it comes to encountering the unexpected, you're not alone. The apostle Paul experienced surprises as well. And one of those surprises turned his life completely around. One minute Paul was going in one direction, and in the next minute, his life was moving totally the opposite direction.

This causes us to wonder, *What happened?*

Paul was a bright and up-and-coming Jewish religious leader. He had an incredible mind and had been tutored by Gamaliel, the great Jewish leader and thinker (Acts 22:3). Yes, the young man Paul was destined to have a great impact upon Judaism. But a radical change took place that he didn't expect. What was it?

## A Dramatic Encounter

Before we see what that surprise was, let's look at what led up to it. What was Paul (called Saul in the verses below) up to?

In the Bible, our first real introduction to Paul is in Acts chapter 9. There we read that "Saul was…breathing out murderous threats against the Lord's disciples." He had even gone to the high priest in Jerusalem and asked for letters to the synagogues in Damascus. Why the letters? So that Paul might take any and all Christians—both male and female— back to Jerusalem as prisoners (Acts 9:1-2).

Here's the scene: Paul was on his way from Jerusalem to Damascus, the ancient capital of Syria, some 100-plus miles to the north. The trek normally took about five or six days. Paul and his henchmen were almost to Damascus. They were within a day's journey. Paul was eager to get to the city and begin dealing with a group he considered to be heretics and a threat to the Jewish faith.

But God had other plans for Paul, the "hit man" for the high priest. "As he neared Damascus on his journey, suddenly a light from heaven flashed around him. He fell to the ground and heard a voice say to him, 'Saul, Saul, why do you persecute me?'"

"Who are you, Lord?" Saul asked.

"'I am Jesus, who you are persecuting,' he replied. 'Now get up and go into the city, and you will be told what you must do'" (Acts 9:3-6).

Needless to say, this dramatic encounter affected Paul's life. Truly, he was never the same! Paul saw, heard, and understood the voice of the Lord. The rest of his companions also saw the bright light and heard something, but they did not understand the voice (Acts 22:9). How can we explain this? We can't. And neither could Paul, who in the years to follow tried to comprehend and write about God's sovereign work in his life. All he could conclude was, "Oh, the depths of the riches of the wisdom and knowledge of God! How unsearchable his judgments, and his paths beyond tracing out!" (Romans 11:33).

## A Sensational Reversal

Somewhere on the road to Damascus, somehow and at some moment (which no one can pinpoint), Paul became saved. He himself became one of those he was persecuting—a Christian. Paul's conversion was definitely dramatic, but the exact moment of salvation cannot be distinguished. Perhaps it was...

> ...when he heard the voice of the Lord,
>
> ...as he lay on the ground,
>
> ...when he was blinded,
>
> ...while he conversed with Christ, or
>
> ...during his three days of prayer and fasting while he awaited God's direction.

Whenever it was, Paul's life was changed so drastically that everyone took note. As you can see in the verses below, people had a hard time understanding Paul's transformation from a persecutor of Christians to a preacher of Christ:

> At once he began to preach in the synagogues that Jesus is the Son of God. All those who heard him were astonished and asked, "Isn't he the man who raised havoc in Jerusalem among those who call on this name? And hasn't he come here to take them as prisoners to the chief priests?" (Acts 9:20-21).

Dear reader, we, along with the people of Damascus, have just witnessed a sensational reversal in Paul's life. Knowing of his past, we are struck by the dramatic change that came over him. Paul went from killing Christians to leading people to Christ. What a complete transformation!

Yes, my friend, prior to this moment, Paul was having an impact. But it was a negative one, not a positive one. His influence went in the wrong direction.

### The Direction of Your Influence

Before we move on, let's pause and ask: What is the direction of your influence? As we move through *The Man Who Makes a Difference,* I will continually remind you to check the direction of your impact and influence. Your influence is never neutral. You are having either a positive or a negative impact on others. In any and all of your relationships, as the following poem states, you are either leading others aright or astray. The choice is yours.

### The Things I Do
The things I do,
The things I say,
Will lead some person
Aright or astray.
So the things we do
Should be the best,
And the things we say
Should be to bless.[2]

### The Dramatic Nature of Your Conversion

The events surrounding Paul's conversion were most definitely out of the ordinary. God used a miraculous event to change the direction of Paul's life. It was so radical that Dr. Charles Swindoll entitled one of his chapters on Paul's life "The Violent Capture of a Rebel's Will."[3]

I don't know about you, but my conversion at the tender age of six didn't have any of the drama associated with Paul's experience. On the surface, you wouldn't describe my conversion as "the violent capture of a rebel's will." It *appears* that I was simply a young boy who needed a Savior and a boy who was fortunate to have a faithful mother who introduced me to that Savior at our family kitchen table while I was at home during my school lunch break.

From time to time, you and I may hear captivating testimonies from people who have been gloriously and dramatically saved from hideous or contrary lifestyles. But, like me, you probably had a conversion that *appears* (there's that word again!) to be a less-than-sensational event.

Well, an "ordinary" conversion may seem an uneventful occurrence on the *human* plane. But, my friend, in the *spiritual* realm, your conversion and mine are anything but ordinary or uneventful! I, like Paul, was a rebel (even at six years old!). And so were you! Our conversion, or re-creation (2 Corinthians 5:17), is an incredible and dramatic event, rivaling even that of Creation itself. And our conversion is just as dynamic as anyone's when we consider these terrifying truths:

- We were spiritually dead in our transgressions and sins (Ephesians 2:1).
- We were children of disobedience—rebels (Ephesians 2:2).
- We were children of wrath (Ephesians 2:3).
- We were separated from Christ (Ephesians 2:12).
- We were without hope and without God in the world (Ephesians 2:12).

We were in a pretty hopeless state. I repeat, we were rebels! We were separated from God on this earth. And to die in this state would mean eternal separation from God. And what's more, *we didn't even care!*

## A Divine Intervention

"But...God" (Ephesians 2:4).

What an incredible statement! *God* initiated a rescue. Paul was on his way to Damascus (and to hell!), doing what he thought was God's will...

"But...God."

Before salvation, you too were on your way through life, hoping, like Paul did, that somehow, in some way, your "good" or "righteous" or "religious" deeds would earn you entrance into God's heaven. But salvation doesn't work that way. *Man's* formula requires man to take the initiative to effect his own salvation. *God's* formula, however, is "But... God." Read it for yourself.

> *But* because of his great love for us, *God,* who is rich in *mercy,* made us alive with Christ even when we were dead in transgressions—it is by *grace* you have been saved (Ephesians 2:4-5).

God's mercy and God's grace intervened in the life of Paul. And God's mercy and God's grace have intervened in your life, too, if you have trusted Christ as your Lord and Savior.

Let's pause again for a moment. What does it mean that God's mercy and grace intervened in our behalf? Remember, you and I were enemies of God (Romans 5:10), just like Paul.

But...God...

- rescued us from the dominion of darkness (Colossians 1:13),
- brought us into the kingdom of the Son (Colossians 1:13),
- saved us through faith (Ephesians 2:8),
- forgave us our sins (Colossians 1:14),
- made us spiritually alive together with Christ (Ephesians 2:5),
- seated us with Him in the heavenly realms in Christ Jesus (Ephesians 2:6), and
- sealed us with the Spirit (2 Corinthians 1:22).

All we can say, along with the hymn writer, is "Hallelujah, what a Savior!"[4]

Now, the next time you hear of someone's "dramatic conversion" or read of a startling salvation experience like Paul's, remember this—you, too, had a dramatic conversion. Remember that Christ's payment for sin was just as great for you as it was for Paul, the rebel, or for any other person who puts their faith in the risen Lord Jesus Christ. *Every* conversion is dramatic! Whether you were a rebel like Paul, or a tender child like Paul's associate Timothy (2 Timothy 1:5), or a hardened warden like the Philippian jailer (Acts 16:29), *every* conversion is dramatic!

## The First Step to a Life of Impact

You know, it just occurred to me that maybe I'm running a bit ahead of you here. Maybe you haven't yet experienced God's grace and mercy in your life. Maybe you haven't received Christ as your Lord and Savior. If not, you can take the first step to a life of influence right now—the same first step Paul had to take—by uttering a heartfelt prayer like this one:

> Jesus, I know I am a sinner. I want to repent of my sins and turn to follow You. I believe You died for my sins and rose again victorious over the power of sin and death, and I want to accept You as my personal Savior. Come into my life, Lord Jesus, and help me obey You from this day forward.

*Truly, opening your heart to Jesus Christ is the first step to a life of influence!* Whether you took that step this moment or at some time in the past, having Jesus Christ as the driving force in your life will ensure that you will have a positive impact on those who come in contact with you.

᠀᠀

Now…back to where we left off with Paul. The great Paul, the persecutor of Christians, was now a believer. Paul was "a new creation." His past was gone—it was history! He had been given a second chance…

and his new life in Christ was ahead of him. Truly, as the Bible explains it, the old was gone and the new had begun (2 Corinthians 5:17).

We must stop and mark this well—Paul's usefulness to God began with his salvation. Every truly godly element of Paul's life, every truly righteous quality, began that day on the Damascus Road. And, my fellow-traveling friend, that's where it begins with you and me as well.

You and I cannot have a godly, righteous influence by our own human efforts. And we cannot have a godly, righteous influence without first meeting the Savior and coming under His influence. I know I am repeating myself, but it's vitally important: Have *you* met the risen Savior, Jesus Christ? Has He given *you* a new beginning? If you want a life of godly impact—a life lived for the glory of God—then you must begin that life with Jesus.

Paul's life of influence was launched when he met the Master face to face on that dusty road to Damascus. And from then on, Paul's life was never the same. Nor is any man who meets Jesus ever the same. You too must meet the Master face to face. That's the first step to a life of impact. As you read the poetic testimony on the next page, ask yourself if you've met the Master.

I had walked life's way with an easy tread,
Had followed where comforts and pleasures led.
Until one day in a quiet place
I met the Master face to face.

With station and rank and wealth for my goal,
Much thought for my body but none for my soul,
I had entered to win in life's mad race,
When I met the Master face to face.

I built my castles and reared them high,
Till their towers had pierced the blue of the sky;
I had sworn to rule with an iron mace,
When I met the Master face to face.

I met Him, and knew Him and blushed to see
That His eyes full of sorrow were fixed on me;
And I faltered and fell at His feet that day,
While my castles melted and vanished away.

Melted and vanished and in their place,
Naught else did I see but the Master's face.
And I cried aloud, "Oh, make me meet
To follow the steps of Thy wounded feet."

My thought is now for the souls of men,
I have lost my life to find it again,
E'er since one day in a quiet place,
I met the Master face to face.[5]

*Key #1*

# The Bible

*It is a thriving soul that finds the Book of God
growing more and more precious.*[1]
—Robert C. Chapman

## 3

# Pursuing a Love for God's Word

*All Scripture is God-breathed
and is useful for teaching, rebuking,
correcting and training in righteousness,
so that the man of God may be thoroughly equipped
for every good work.*
—2 TIMOTHY 3:16-17

No man lives in a vacuum. We are all influenced and impacted by our surroundings. Every man can point to someone or something that shaped his life in some way or another, for either good or bad. For some it might even have been a combination of someones and somethings.

Obviously parents contribute much toward making us the men we are today. But beyond that, can you think of someone who has impacted you, and to what extent and in what direction? Was it a teacher, a coach, a pastor? For some it wasn't a person but a life-altering experience, such as a brush with death during a tour of duty in a war zone or maybe a life-threatening accident or illness. For me it was an event. It was when I finally realized that the Bible was different from any other book in the world. What was amazing is I had already been told this very truth all my Christian life. What led up to this moment of truth? Let me explain.

## One Man's Example and Impact

Influence isn't about numbers. No, it's about individuals. Individuals with a passion, a focus, or an intensity—or all of the above—that drives them forward. It's this energy that attracts a following. Most men of influence down through the centuries have gained their influence through a crisis, cause, or mandate. In the case of the apostle Paul, there was a mandate from God to take the gospel to the Gentiles.

From the first time I heard John MacArthur preach from God's Word and observed how he viewed the importance of correctly understanding the meaning of Scripture, I saw a man on a mission. His desire was that people would develop a love for the Bible and understand how important it is to the life and faithfulness of every Christian.

As I said earlier, I was one of the countless Christians who had never given much thought about their Bible. I, like so many others, knew many of the Bible stories but never saw their connection to my life. I also didn't have much to do with my Bible. Oh, I was given a Bible when I was young, and I dutifully carried it to church every Sunday. But I never grasped the importance of the Bible. It wasn't until I observed the power and authority of the Bible on John MacArthur's life and ministry that I longed to know his secret and the reasons for his convictions about the Bible and life. The influence of this one man and his belief in the importance of God's Word had an impact on my life.

It was John's love for God's Word that attracted me to my Bible. His focus and intensity inspired me to look into the Bible for myself. That was the beginning of a love relationship with my Bible. John's stress on the centrality of Scripture in all of life has not only affected me, but countless thousands of others who have sat under his teaching, heard him on the radio, listened to his tapes and CDs, studied through his New Testament commentaries, or used his study Bible. I still feel John's impact on my life today, 35 years after first hearing him teach and sensing his belief in the grandness of God's Word. I'm still being shaped by his example, and now my desire is to pass this love for God's Word on to you!

So as we continue our study of the keys that give a man credibility, that make him a person of influence, especially as a Christian man, we must try and understand why the Bible is so important in the development of that influence.

In this chapter I'll share some reasons the Bible is an essential part of becoming a man who makes a difference. Then in the next chapter I'll explain how the Bible prepares you to have a meaningful impact on others.

## What's So Special About the Bible?

At first glance, the Bible looks and feels like any other book. The pages have printed words, like any other book or magazine, or even a newspaper. And yet the Bible is very special for a number of reasons. For one, it has survived countless attempts to destroy it. Then there are the claims that people make about it.

### David's Claims About the Bible

In Acts 13, we find the apostle Paul preaching to a group of people and giving them a history lesson on God's dealings with Israel. He speaks of how King Saul was set aside and why God chose David to take Saul's place. God gives David's qualification for the job, explaining, "I have found David son of Jesse a man after my own heart; he will do everything I want him to do" (verse 22). That's quite a commendation! How do you think David was able to fulfill God's will? Obviously, he had to *know* God's will before he could *do* God's will.

In Psalm 19:7-11, David gave us a hint of what he used to determine God's will. This is what he claimed about the Bible:

—*It is the perfect law.* The Bible has no errors. It gives an accurate account of historical fact and provides spiritual truth (verse 7).

—*It is a sure testimony.* The truths of the Bible do not change. It is God's testimony of what is true and right (verse 7).

—*It is a rule book for daily living.* Some man-made rules are wrong, but God's Word is always 100 percent right (verse 8).

—*It is a pure commandment.* Nothing in the Bible, rightly understood, could ever lead a person into sin. In fact, Scripture does just the opposite. It leads people out of sin and into purity (verse 8).

—*It is eternal.* Other books come and go, but the Bible endures forever (verse 9).

—*It is a treasure.* Gold is valuable, but the Bible has greater value. It contains everything that pertains to life and godliness (2 Peter 1:3). What's more valuable than that (verse 10)?

David also tells us what the Bible does:

—*It refreshes and heals.* The Word of God converts the sinner from his ways and restores the saint when he wanders (verse 7).

—*It makes its readers wise.* Even an uneducated man can become wise by reading the Bible (verse 7).

—*It gladdens the heart.* When a person reads the Bible his heart finds joy (verse 8).

—*It illuminates the mind.* The Bible gives meaning to life (verse 8).

—*It enriches.* It is better than gold or silver (verse 10).

—*It satisfies.* As food satisfies the body, the Word of the Lord satisfies a man's soul (verse 10).

—*It warns.* Knowing the Word and obeying it guides the believer on the safe path (verse 11).

—*It rewards.* There is no greater reward than a clean conscience, a pure heart, and peace of mind. This kind of reward does not come from knowing God's Word, but from *keeping* it. The reward comes in the doing (verse 11; see also James 1:25).

No one doubts that David was a man after God's own heart. He was a man God used mightily. He made an impact on others. Judging from his claims about the Bible, we can see where he got his instruction, his wisdom, his power, and his focus to lead God's people.

### Paul's Claims About the Bible

Paul was a student of the Old Testament long before he became a Christian. He had been taught by the great Old Testament scholar Gamaliel (Acts 22:3). So when Jesus met Paul on the road to Damascus and commissioned him to take God's Word to the Gentiles, Paul already had a knowledge of God. But the Holy Spirit enlightened that knowledge during a private time in the desert.

Later Paul wrote to Timothy, his young disciple, and gave a great testimony about the origin and character of the Bible in 2 Timothy 3:16-17.

—*The Bible has a divine origin.* The Bible is the inspired Word of God. The word *inspired* means God-breathed, filled with the breath of God. The Spirit of God enabled men of God to write the Word of God. Not just certain books of the Bible, but "all Scripture is inspired by God" (verse 16 NASB).

—*The Bible has a divine purpose.* What is the purpose of the Bible (verses 16-17)?

*Salvation* is the one primary purpose as seen in the life of Timothy (verse 15).

*Sanctification* is a second purpose (verse 16). Godly Christian living is the significant result of reading, studying, and obeying the Bible.

- The Word is beneficial for teaching the precepts or doctrines of God.

- It convicts us of sin.

- It corrects our wrong thinking.

- It instructs us in godly living and discipline.

- It matures our childish thinking and makes us men of God who are sensitive to the things of God (verse 17).

The great need among churches and Christians in Paul's day was that people would not neglect to read and study God's Word. They needed to grasp the supernatural nature of God's Word in their lives. That's why Paul reminded Timothy of its importance in 2 Timothy 3:16-17. Then Paul began chapter four with a charge to Timothy to focus his attention on preaching and teaching the Word of God in its entirety. "Preach the Word," Paul exhorted. Because "all Scripture is God-breathed," all Scripture must be taught so that nothing is left out for personal application.

Paul modeled this commitment to teaching the entire body of Scripture when he reminded the Ephesian elders that he had not "shunned to declare to [them] the whole counsel of God" (Acts 20:27 NKJV).

### An Unnamed Author's Claims About the Bible

The book of Hebrews was written to Jewish Christians after Paul's death. They were facing intense persecution, which led them to waver in their faith. The author emphasized the superiority of Christianity over Judaism and the superiority of Christ over the inferior Levitical sacrifices observed at the temple in Jerusalem. The question of the day was, Were those who were wavering really true believers? The author claimed that God's Word was alive and exposed the true nature of their faith:

> The word of God is living and powerful, and sharper than any two-edged sword, piercing even to the division of soul and spirit, and of joints and marrow, and is a discerner of the thoughts and intents of the heart (Hebrews 4:12 NKJV).

Here the Scripture claims to be the Word of God, a true and faithful message, and to be alive and able to judge our thoughts and the attitudes of our hearts.

Can you see why gaining a love and appreciation for the Bible is important for a man who wants to make an impact on the world around him? Let's recap.

David was a man after God's own heart, a man who knew and loved Scripture and obeyed it. Obviously David wasn't perfect. God wasn't looking for that in David. God was looking for—and found—spiritual growth and progress.

Paul too was a man with a deep love, respect, and appreciation for God's Word. He lived out his commitment to Scripture and took its message and focus to the far reaches of the Roman Empire. He attracted others who responded to this same focus. He, like Timothy, Titus, and others, responded to his conviction, and they in turn spread out to the four corners of the Roman Empire with these same claims.

## Developing a Passion for the Bible

My hope is that David, Paul, and present-day men with a passion for God's Word will inspire you to look more closely at the claims of Scripture. So that you too can develop a consuming passion for God's Word, here are some suggestions:

—*Recognize the supernatural nature of Scripture.* The Bible is the foundation of belief. Jesus claimed to be God and the Savior of the world. You can't see Him, but you believe in Him. The Bible doesn't look different, but it claims to be written by God, to be alive, to contain everything you need for living in a godly way (2 Peter 1:3). By faith you need to recognize and accept the Bible as your greatest resource.

—*Read and study Scripture.* Once you're ready to accept the Bible, then you need to allow it to work in your life. It will give you the wisdom, maturity, and power for living a victorious Christian life. As Paul told his disciple Timothy, "Be diligent to present yourself approved to God as a workman who does not need to be ashamed, accurately handling the word of truth" (2 Timothy 2:15 NASB). Once you heed this admonition from Paul, your life will become something others want— and want to follow.

—*Respond to Scripture.* Paul admonished his Colossian readers to "let the word of Christ dwell in you richly" (Colossians 3:16). Scripture can and should infuse every aspect of your life and control every thought, word, and deed. God didn't give us the Ten Suggestions. He gave the Ten Commandments. As you well know, a command is meant to be obeyed.

—*Resolve to live out Scripture.* Obedience to the commands in the Bible leads to righteous living. This is a tall order in today's immoral society. It's never been easy to live for God—not in Paul's day, nor during any other period in Christian history. And guess what? It isn't easy today either. God wants you to be His man, a man who makes a difference. And He's given you the resources to be His man. When you respond to God and you allow His Word to fill you, the Holy Spirit will empower you to become the bold influence you need to be.

In the next chapter we'll take this key to impacting others a step further and hopefully commit ourselves even more sincerely to ensuring that the Word of Christ dwells in us richly (Colossians 3:16). This kind of commitment to the Bible is vitally important for a man who wants to make a difference in his family, the community, and the world.

*The Bible was written not to be studied but to change*
*our lives. Life-change is the product we are after.*
*The human heart resists nothing more than change,*
*but spiritual growth is a commitment to change.*[1]
—HOWARD G. HENDRICKS

# Persevering for Life

*When your words came, I ate them;*
*they were my joy and my heart's delight,*
*for I bear your name, O LORD God Almighty.*

—JEREMIAH 15:16

B ecause of my passion for church history, I can't resist sharing a bit of it here as you and I continue to consider just how important it is to have a love for the Bible, which is the first key to a life of impact.

John Wycliffe, a teacher of theology at Oxford University in the fourteenth century, gave us a notable illustration of the importance of a love for God's Word. In his day, Wycliffe was one of the few who declared that the Scriptures are the authoritative center of Christianity. Wycliffe was called the morning star of the Reformation because he was one of the earliest opponents of papal authority, and an early advocate for translating the Bible into the language of the people. Until an English translation was completed in 1382, only those who could read Latin had a chance at understanding the Bible.

In spite of the zeal with which the church hierarchy sought to destroy Wycliffe's English translations (due to what the church perceived as mistranslations and erroneous commentary), there still exist today about 150 manuscripts, complete or partial, of Wycliffe's translation in its revised form. From the number of manuscripts still available after hundreds of years, scholars believe the breadth of this translation's impact was widespread on the people of England. Those who preached and taught from this version were called "Wycliffites" in England and were often designated by their opponents as "Bible men."

Even after his death, John Wycliffe's translation was condemned. But just as Martin Luther's version had great influence upon the German language, so Wycliffe's work, by reason of its clarity, beauty, and strength, affected the English people and the English language in much the same way the King James Version would almost 300 years later.

## The Influence of God's Word

You may have tens or even a hundred or more books on your shelves at home. But the Bible stands above and apart from all other books. I repeat, it is like no other book. Church history is filled with men like John Wycliffe and Martin Luther, who recognized the uniqueness of the Bible and championed for it to become available in their own language. They understood the importance of making it possible for people to read the Bible for themselves. These great men of influence believed the claims of the Bible. They knew this special book was spiritually alive and able to change lives. They were also willing to make sacrifices to see that the Bible got into the hands of the people.

Do you believe that the Bible is God's Word, alive, and a force for change in your life? Are you ready to find out how it can transform you into the kind of man God can use to influence others for Him? If so, then you are ready to take the next step. Step one is to believe in the power and uniqueness of the Bible. And step two is to accept and obey its commands.

### The Bible Will Lead You to Salvation

If you and I are to become men of impact, salvation must be the starting point as it was in the life of the apostle Paul. Paul met Jesus on the road to Damascus. We meet Jesus in the Bible. The Old Testament prophesies His coming. The Gospels speak of His sinless life and substitutionary death. And the New Testament epistles instruct us on what it means to believe in Jesus for eternal life. Paul reminded Timothy of this quality when he said,

> As for you, continue in what you have learned and have become convinced of, because you know those from whom you learned it, and how from infancy you have known the holy Scriptures, which are able to make you wise for salvation through faith in Christ Jesus (2 Timothy 3:14-15).

The apostle James made a similar claim about the Bible when he said,

> Get rid of all moral filth and the evil that is so prevalent and humbly accept the word planted in you, which can save you (James 1:21).

As we're addressing salvation through Christ, if you are at all unsure of what salvation means and how you can make it personal, reread the chapter "Taking the First Step." It's vital that you make sure you are starting with Jesus Christ as your focus and the source of all the influence you will ever have in the lives of others.

### The Bible Will Give You Success

A significant challenge of becoming someone who makes a difference is that it requires credibility. It requires success. No one wants to follow a "loser." Maybe that's why there are so many books written on the topic of success. They all promise steps or ways or secrets to obtaining success. But the only true way to success is found in God's message

to Joshua when the nation of Israel was about to enter the Promised
Land:

> Do not let this Book of the Law depart from your mouth;
> meditate on it day and night, so that you may be careful
> to do everything written in it. Then you will be prosper-
> ous and successful (Joshua 1:8-9).

"You will be prosperous and successful." What a promise! Did you
notice the four keys to this promise?

Key #1: Believe in the Bible— *"this Book of the Law"*
The Bible isn't some sort of magical book. Merely reading it doesn't
make you successful. But do you believe it to be divine truth? Do you
believe that God and His Word are the beginning of a life of blessing,
the starting point for success in all that really matters? If you do, then
trust that God will bless your efforts and your endeavors.

Key #2: Talk About the Bible— *"Do not let this Book...depart from
your mouth"*
To talk about something, you have to know about it first. God
wants you to know success. But He also wants others to know where
your success comes from. As you get into the habit of reading your
Bible, God will give you plenty of opportunities to share with others
the things you are learning.

Key #3: Study the Bible— *"meditate on it day and night"*
You cannot correctly do or follow what you don't understand. You
must understand the Bible in your mind before it can move your heart
and change your life.

Key #4: Obey the Bible— *"so that you may be careful to do everything
written in it"*
It's easy to read a principle or a command in the Bible. The hard
part is obeying God's commands. God promises that when we follow
His precepts, He will lead us into a successful life. This does not nec-
essarily refer to financial success or wealth, but success where it really

matters—in the spiritual realm. God will bless you with success in your relationships with your wife, children, employer, and countless others whom your life touches.

### The Bible Will Change Your Attitude

Jeremiah was God's prophet during the last days of the kingdom of Judah. God had commissioned him to bring a message of doom to the people. They had rejected both God and His Word. Therefore God would send them into exile in the land of Babylon. During a particularly dark point in Jeremiah's ministry, he felt the hatred and rejection the people had toward him because of his unpopular message. At that time Jeremiah uttered words of dejection. He displayed a "poor me" attitude. He even wished he had never been born. Why? Because of his message of coming judgment, everyone saw him as a "man of strife and a man of contention to the whole earth!" (15:10 NKJV). The Lord responded to Jeremiah's lament with a promise of protection (verses 11-14).

But in the midst of this self-pity, Jeremiah's thinking appears to take a turn. He evidently picked up a scroll of some portion of the Old Testament and, in response to what he read, he lifted up a prayer for renewed strength. His response to God flowed out of three convictions he felt:

*A positive response to God's word.* "Your words were found, and I ate them, and Your word was to me the joy and rejoicing of my heart" (verse 16 NKJV). Jeremiah was basically responding to God's message and consumed it just as one eats and digests a meal. The assimilated words of God did a work within him, and his attitude changed from one of self-absorption and self-pity to bold confidence.

*A renewed sense of God's call.* "For I am called by Your name, O LORD God of hosts" (verse 16 NKJV). Jeremiah had become resolved, even in the midst of rejection, to renew his firm belief in the call God had placed on his life (see 1:4-10). Not only was Jeremiah called, but he was called by the One whose name is above all names and who is in control over all things.

*A resolve to stand alone.* "I did not sit in the assembly of the mockers, nor did I rejoice; I sat alone because of Your hand, for you have filled me with indignation" (verse 17 NKJV). Jeremiah paid the price for all-out discipleship, for following God with a whole heart. He did not sit as a compromiser, joining those who were committed to their own merry way, those under a delusion.

To help Jeremiah stand strong, God had filled him with His Word. This restored Jeremiah's submission to proclaiming God's message of judgment. Jeremiah's encounter with God and God's Word was a true watershed event. At times, when things got even more desperate, Jeremiah almost faltered. But to the end he never gave up, thanks to the grace of the ministry of God's Word in his heart.

### The Bible Will Change You in Many Ways

If you aren't satisfied with the way you're acting or living, the Bible can definitely help you. There's no way to adequately describe all the ways God's Word can change you. But a good starting point for you is to ask yourself, Where is change most needed? Here's an abbreviated list of the power of God's Word to effect change. This list only scratches the surface, for there are many more ways His Word can bring change. Just start reading your Bible and you'll start changing!

- The Bible can equip you for every good work (2 Timothy 3:17).
- The Bible can stimulate your spiritual growth (Acts 20:32).
- The Bible can give you wisdom (Proverbs 4:11).
- The Bible can give you peace (Proverbs 3:1-2 NKJV).
- The Bible can give you direction (Psalm 119:105).
- The Bible can keep you from sin (Psalm 119:11).

- The Bible can give you power (Colossians 1:11).
- The Bible can give you discernment for godly living (Hebrews 5:14).

Notice I didn't say, "The Bible *will…*" I said, "The Bible *can…*" All the power and potential you need for change and growth is available…*when* you look to God's Word, learn God's Word, and keep God's Word.

There's not a parent alive who doesn't desire physical growth for their children. It's always a great tragedy to see a physical illness or disability hinder the growth of a beloved son or daughter. And it's the same in the spiritual realm. God, your heavenly Father, desires that you grow spiritually. The following verses show us God's desire and commands for spiritual growth:

> Rid yourselves of all malice and all deceit, hypocrisy, envy, and slander of every kind. Like newborn babies, crave pure spiritual milk, so that by it you may grow up in your salvation (1 Peter 2:1-2).

> Grow in the grace and knowledge of our Lord and Savior Jesus Christ. To him be glory both now and forever! Amen (2 Peter 3:18).

> Speaking the truth in love, we will in all things grow up into him who is the Head, that is, Christ (Ephesians 4:15).

Do you share in God's desire for your growth? God won't force growth upon you. You must desire it enough to do something about it. As you look at your own heart, what is the burning desire of your soul? Do you truly want to be God's man who makes a difference, who has a positive, dynamic impact on those around him? I hope you're saying, "Yes! I want to grow spiritually. I want my life to have a positive impact on others. I want to be God's man."

## Becoming God's Man

So where and how do you begin? Here are some steps you can take:

1. *Desire to follow Jesus.* Hopefully you have already taken the first step toward a life of impact by receiving Jesus Christ as your personal Savior. If not, now is a good time to do so. Keep in mind that a true follower doesn't merely follow Christ only when it's convenient. We're called to full-time faithfulness without hesitation or reservation. This is what Jesus asked of His disciples 2000 years ago, and He's asking it of you and me today: "If anyone would come after me, he must deny himself and take up his cross *daily* and follow me" (Luke 9:23).

2. *Grapple with sin.* Even as Christians we will struggle against the temptation to fall into sin. We will experience a constant battle with the flesh and its desires and passions, which go against God's standards as stated in the Bible. If we do sin, we cannot ignore the sin, like David did when he tried to hide his affair with Bathsheba (2 Samuel 11). For about one year David kept silent about his wrongdoing. As a result he suffered some very real physical side effects. You can read the description of his agony in Psalm 32:3-5, where David said he was groaning, sapped, heavy, and wasted away.

Unconfessed sin always hinders and stifles your spiritual growth. So to ensure that your growth remains steady and uninterrupted, keep a short record of sins with God. Confess any and all sins to Him right away. If you want to experience a close, ongoing relationship with God, do as David finally did and confess your sins, whether big or small. Make confession a habit so you can experience the wonderful cleansing that comes afterwards. David sends this message to us, written after his confession: "Blessed is he whose transgressions are forgiven, whose sins are covered" (Psalm 32:1).

3. *Refuse to be spiritually lazy.* Life is full of choices. Each day you must choose what you will or won't do. Will you exercise today to keep yourself fit? Will you stick to your diet? Will you use your free time to work on a hobby or watch another three hours of television? These

decisions relating to your physical health will affect the quality of your life. You must make even more serious choices when it come to the spiritual realm. Will you read your Bible and pray today? Will you deal with that unconfessed sin? Your choices will determine whether you grow spiritually strong or become spiritually lazy.

Just as laziness is a sin and unproductive for you personally, so being spiritually lazy has its consequences. Why not ask the Lord right now—and every day—to help you make choices that will promote your spiritual development and increase your impact for Christ on others?

4. *Find a role model.* It's often said that a picture is worth a thousand words. Well, look around for a "picture" of a man who's making a difference, a mature-in-the-Lord man who can mentor you and provide you with counsel, guidance, and encouragement on a regular basis. That is exactly what I did as a young and spiritually immature man, husband, and dad. Oh, I'd been a Christian since an early age, but I had never grown in the things of the Lord. Over the years I've met with many different men who have helped me mature—men who have lived out the "Timothy Principle" in 2 Timothy 2:2.

5. *Realize that spiritual growth is ongoing.* Just as God's people had to daily gather manna, the food God provided for them while they were in the wilderness, so spiritual growth must be pursued daily. The manna never lasted beyond the day it was given, and when it comes to spiritual maturity, you cannot rest or count on yesterday's growth. You may think you can get by without reading your Bible, praying, and being accountable for your walk with God. But without ongoing spiritual nourishment, you'll wake up one day and find yourself defeated in your Christian walk.

Don't try to slide by on yesterday's growth. Get the help you need. Find the resources that will educate and stimulate ongoing growth. Dedicate yourself to growing spiritually every single day for the rest of your life. Then you *will* become a man who makes a difference.

*Key #2*

# Prayer

*Prayer is a spiritual discipline that is difficult for even the most devout Christian to practice on a truly consistent basis. It demands time and requires focus, which are hard for modern minds and lifestyles to incorporate. To pray also requires us to overcome our natural tendency to try and come up with our own solutions. Prayer tries our patience. We dislike waiting on God's answers. So we try to manipulate our situation by coming up with our own quick answers.* [1]

—JIM GEORGE

# Understanding the Significance of Prayer

*Ask, and it will be given to you;*
*seek, and you will find;*
*knock, and the door will be opened to you.*
*For everyone who asks receives;*
*he who seeks finds;*
*and to him who knocks, the door will be opened.*
—Matthew 7:7-8

The apostle Paul was a man of action. He was a man's man, a leader's leader, and a teacher's teacher. He was smart and well-educated. In today's vernacular, Paul would be considered a type A personality. He could do it all himself. He could stand before a group of Greek philosophers in Athens and debate with the best of them. And he could stand before kings and speak with such confidence that his royal audience would walk away amazed.

From a human perspective Paul was self-sufficient and highly competent. So most people might be surprised to learn that Paul was a great advocate of complete dependence upon God in prayer. This dependence goes against all the rules for a SNL (Strong Natural Leader). A SNL takes charge and is at his best as he makes unilateral decisions based on his own abilities. But prayer, by its very definition, looks to a higher power for wisdom and direction. Paul recognized that his usefulness to God was in direct proportion to his dependence on God. And because Paul was useful to God, he couldn't help but make a difference in his world. That's why prayer is such a vital key to a life of impact!

## The Characteristics of Prayer

### Prayer Is Talking to God

Communication is a two-way street. It requires active participation by two people. In the case of God and His people, He communicates to us through His Word, and we respond to Him in prayer. Which may explain one reason we're sometimes hesitant to pray. We have nothing to say because we haven't listened to what God has said to us in His Word. Or we have issues we aren't willing to deal with—areas of sin and disobedience we don't want to admit. We're reluctant to meet with God through His Word because we know it will point out the thoughts and intents of our heart (Hebrews 4:12).

Because communication requires two people, we need to show a willingness to communicate with God. He has already communicated with us, and we need to make the effort to connect with Him.

### Prayer Is an Act of Faith

When you pray to God, you are talking to someone you can't see, someone whose existence is tangibly validated only by what you see of His handiwork in creation (Romans 1:20) or of the revelation of Himself in the Bible. So prayer is the purest form of faith, which is described as "being sure of what we hope for and certain of what we do not see" (Hebrews 11:1). Yet the faith of prayer is not based on vivid imagination or wishful thinking. It is based on the promises of God, which are found in the Bible.

When the apostle Paul was arrested and taken by ship to Rome, he was chained to a Roman soldier the entire way. When a severe storm hit their small boat in the Mediterranean Sea, all hope seemed to be lost. But Paul stood before the wet and discouraged passengers and crew and reported that an angel of God had appeared to him and declared that he, Paul, would go on to stand before Caesar. With confidence Paul exhorted, "So keep up your courage, men, for I have faith in God that it will happen just as he told me" (Acts 27:26).

While we don't have angels standing beside us today to reassure us when things get rough, we do have the assurances in the Bible, which are 100 percent faithful and true. Therefore, we can pray with confidence and in complete faith that God will keep the promises He has made to us.

### Prayer Seeks the Will of God

Wouldn't it be incredible to know God's will for your life as you make every decision? Imagine having no more guesswork. Instead, you'd have perfect direction each and every time! Unfortunately, only one man accomplished that feat—the Lord Jesus Christ. His decisions were not clouded by the presence of sin in His life. That's because He was sinless and God in human flesh. Yet in humility, Jesus always sought the Father's will through prayer. He consulted with His Father before beginning His day (Mark 1:35), and communed with Him throughout His day and even sometimes all night long—especially before He made important decisions, such as choosing His disciples (Luke 6:12-13).

Jesus' desire to follow the Father's divine will was especially evident the night before His death as He lay prostrate on the ground praying, "O My Father, if it is possible, let this cup pass from Me; nevertheless, not as I will, but as You will" (Matthew 26:39 NKJV). That night He uttered this same prayer two more times. Why did He repeat the prayer? Jesus wasn't in conflict with the divine will. No, His conflict came as He wrestled in His humanity with what He knew He had to do—fulfill the Father's will and pay the price for sinners by dying a painful death on the cross.

Prayer is our attempt to bring our wills and desires in line with the divine will. How can we make sure we don't misinterpret God as we pray? There are two helps we have when we pray to know God's will.

Help #1—the Holy Spirit. The Holy Spirit is the resident truth teacher promised by Jesus in John 14:16-17. His job is to enlighten believers in spiritual matters like prayer.

> The Spirit helps us in our weakness. We do not know what we ought to pray for, but the Spirit himself inter-cedes for us with groans that words cannot express. And he who searches our hearts knows the mind of the Spirit, because the Spirit intercedes for the saints in accordance with God's will (Romans 8:26-27).

The Holy Spirit is available to intercede for us, but there's one big glaring problem—sin. Two verses describe the effects of sin on the ministry of the Spirit. One tells us, "Do not grieve the Holy Spirit" (Ephesians 4:30), and the other warns, "Do not quench the Spirit" (1 Thessalonians 5:19 NKJV). So if you and I are to seek God's will through prayer, we need to come into His presence with a "clean slate." We need to make sure we've dealt with any recent sin and areas of dis-obedience in our lives.

Help #2—The Word of God. God's will is revealed in the Bible. He makes clear what He desires from us. As I said earlier about the Ten Commandments, God didn't give us the Ten Suggestions. He gave us *commands.* Here's how the psalmist described the way the Word directs us into the will of God: "Your word is a lamp to my feet and a light for my path" (Psalm 119:105).

### Prayer Is a Privilege

Historically and even today, it's very rare for everyday people to have the opportunity to speak to important persons like kings, presidents, political leaders, or the CEOs of big corporations. Yet amazingly the God of the universe encourages us to come confidently before His throne to receive mercy and grace in times of need (Hebrews 4:16). What a privilege He offers us! It's truly amazing that our Father in heaven wants to hear from us. He actually wants us to share our problems with Him. In an age when so many don't want to take the time to stop and listen, it's reassuring to know that God is always available and ready to hear from us.

### Prayer Is Hard to Comprehend

Elizabeth and I live in the beautiful backwoods of the Olympic Peninsula in Washington state. Our house is on a hill and has several levels. I write on one level and she writes on another. When our grandkids come over they always want to play with the walkie-talkies that Elizabeth and I use to communicate with each other. And right on cue, after several minutes of attempting to use the walkie-talkies, they come to me complaining that the devices are broken. Because they are too young to understand how to send and receive messages, Jacob and Katie—or Taylor and Mattie—are sure the problem has to do with the walkie-talkies.

Friend, we sometimes do the same when it comes to prayer. When we think our prayers aren't being answered, we tend to get discouraged and blame God. We think He is the problem. We cry out, "Why isn't God answering my prayers?"

Yet God has promised to answer our prayers, and He always comes through:

> Ask and it will be given to you;
> seek and you will find;
> knock and the door will be opened to you.
> For everyone who asks receives;
> he who seeks finds;
> and to him who knocks, the door will be opened
> (Matthew 7:7-8).

God does answer our prayers! In fact, He promises to answer us when we pray. However, sometimes we don't see the answer for a while, or God may answer no because He has a different—and better—plan.

God also answers even when we don't know how to pray about a certain issue. When that happens, the Holy Spirit steps in and "intercedes for us" (Romans 8:26). He helps us to pray when we're unsure of what to pray for.

So God asks us to *ask*. But keep in mind that your request must be...

in faith (Matthew 21:22),
without selfish motives (James 4:3), and
according to the will of God (1 John 5:14-15).

## The Problem of Prayer

Clearly, prayer is vital if we're going to have a life of impact. Yet why do many of us have such a hard time with prayer? We'll continue to look at the importance of prayer in the next chapter. For now, let's pause and look at two questions many men ask about prayer.

### 1. Why do we have such a hard time with prayer?

The answer may lie in the fact that most men seem to have difficulty asking—asking for directions, asking for help of any kind, and specifically, asking for help from God! In general, we as men simply are reluctant to ask. Therefore, we don't see God at work with His answers—not only in our lives, but also in the lives of our family and a host of others. We're not as attuned to what God is doing.

### 2. Why don't we pray more often?

Well, we've hit the jackpot on this one! Here are at least nine reasons we don't pray more often. Feel free to add to the list as you read along.

*Worldliness*—We live in a world where there is no voice admonishing us to pray. Prayer is a spiritual exercise. Therefore, we must take the initiative to be spiritually minded. Yes we are *in* the world, but we are not to be *of* the world (John 17:16). We must ask for spiritual assistance to develop a heart for prayer.

*Busyness*—We think we are so busy that we can't take time to stop and pray. Yet we are never too busy to play golf, go fishing or hunting, work on a hobby, or sit for three-plus hours watching our favorite sports team on television. We are never too busy to do the things that we think are important. Yet isn't prayer—and time with God—more important than all those other things?

*Faithlessness*—For whatever reason, we doubt that things might actually have a different outcome due to faithful and earnest prayer on our part. But if we had confidence and believed that God answers prayer, we wouldn't be able to wait to come into His presence with our needs and requests! We'd be asking for—and enjoying—God's answers! When we don't see God at work in our lives, perhaps it's because we fail to pray: "You do not have, because you do not ask" (James 4:2).

*Distance*—When we fail to pray, we'll end up feeling distant from God. And that, in turn, makes us even more reluctant to pray. Though we may feel distant, God is actually close by. He hasn't changed, moved, disappeared, or lost interest in you. Close the gap. Take a simple step toward God and talk to Him. The more you talk to God, the more comfortable you'll become communicating with Him. And the more you communicate, the more opportunity you'll have to ask for His help for yourself and on behalf of others. And the more you ask, the more answers and guidance you'll receive.

*Ignorance*—If we don't read our Bibles or pray, we won't understand God's power and goodness. We won't grasp His desire and His ability to provide "exceeding abundantly above all that we ask or think" (Ephesians 3:20 NKJV), and to "supply all of [our] need" (Philippians 4:19 NKJV). If we knew God better, we would take time to pray.

*Sinfulness*—We allow sin to build a barrier between us and a caring

God. What did the psalmist say? "If I regard iniquity in my heart, the Lord will not hear" (Psalm 66:18 NKJV). But when we confess our sin, the Lord's ears are open to our cries (Psalm 34:15). Don't let sin get in the way of your communication with God!

*Pridefulness*—We, in essence, say to God, "I don't need You. I can take care of this myself. No thanks!" Think about this: "The self-sufficient do not pray, the self-satisfied will not pray, the self-righteous cannot pray."[2] Please don't ever become too proud to pray!

*Inexperience*—We don't pray; therefore, we don't know how to pray...so we don't pray! Prayer is like any skill—it becomes easier with repetition. The more we pray, the more we become comfortable with prayer and know how to pray. And the more we pray, the more answers to prayer we experience!

*Laziness*—Maybe this is the saddest excuse of all. We're just not willing to make the effort to pray, no matter how important it is... which, of course, affects our chances of having our prayers answered. *Lord, may we never get to this place in our spiritual life!*

Did any of those reasons speak to you? (I know I got hit by one or two myself as I just read through this chapter again!) If you're like me, you know when you aren't praying like you should. Once you've identified your problem areas, get to work and tackle them. Prayer is a vital key in the life of a man who makes a difference.

Now let's take prayer to the next level...by doing something about it. Read on!

*Paul's course was more distinctly shaped
and his career rendered more powerfully successful
by prayer than by any other force.*[1]
—E.M. BOUNDS

# Participating in a Life of Prayer

*Do not be anxious about anything, but in everything,
by prayer and petition, with thanksgiving,
present your requests to God.*

—Philippians 4:6

There's no doubt the apostle Paul was a man who made a difference in his day. And it's no secret that his influence has extended far beyond his day down through the centuries to you and me and the church today. And there is plenty of evidence in the Bible of the value Paul placed on prayer. As you read the New Testament you'll discover that the theme and practice of prayer are generously sprinkled throughout the 13 epistles Paul penned. His focus on prayer begins to show up in his earlier letters, which were written to the Thessalonian church. He says he and others are praying for the church, "making mention of you in our prayers, remembering without ceasing" (1 Thessalonians 1:2-3). This focus on prayer seems to increase as Paul continues throughout his life and ministry. It seems that the more involved Paul became in the Lord's work, the more he participated in a life of prayer.

## Praying in the Midst of a Busy Life

Paul's prayer life is most evident in the epistles he wrote while in prison. Some people might assume that confinement in prison gave Paul little choice but to pray. They would imagine Paul saying, "Oh well, since I have nothing else to do, I guess I'll pray." Not true!

As we saw in the last chapter, busyness is often used as an excuse not to pray. But in reality, it's not our schedule that keeps us from praying. It's our failure to understand the importance of prayer. When we don't pray, it's because we don't believe it's all that necessary for us to do so. Instead of utilizing the power of prayer to make an impact, we try to have an influence through physical activity. We roll up our sleeves and get busy, turning to our own power instead of God's power.

It's true that both a commitment to prayer and some muscle are needed among Christians today. In fact, Paul himself would whole-heartedly agree. He definitely spent a lot of time "in the trenches" confronting sorcery, angry mobs, and hostile religious leaders. But that didn't divert his thinking about the need for prayer. Martin Luther, the great church reformer, captured the essence of Paul's prayer philosophy with this paraphrased quote: "My schedule is so busy today that I need to spend more time than usual in prayer."

Paul's—and Martin Luther's—message to us is, "Don't let a busy life keep you from prayer. You need prayer!" And, like the people whom Paul prayed for, others need your prayers as well. And who knows? Maybe the reason your own life is so busy and often out of control is because you don't take the time to stop and pray to discern God's priorities in your life.

## Praying for Direction

I'm sure you've heard the saying, "If you don't know where you're going, then any road will get you there." A man who doesn't know where he's going will have very little positive influence on others. Most people are already clueless about which direction to go, so they absolutely don't need another person who doesn't know where he's going telling them to go in the same direction—which is *no* direction.

From the moment of his conversion on the road to Damascus, Paul sought his Savior's direction. As Paul shook in fear and shielded his eyes from the blinding radiance of Christ's glory, he asked, "Lord, what do You want me to do?" At that moment Paul was given his first instructions by Jesus: "Arise and go into the city, and you will be told what you must do" (Acts 9:6 NKJV).

Praying for direction doesn't always mean you will receive a complete set of instructions right away. If you truly want to rely on the wisdom and direction of God, then prayers for guidance and direction will become part of your everyday life. And you'll wait patiently as God, over time, makes His direction known to you.

Let's return to Paul's conversion. We next see him sitting in a house on "Straight Street." What is he doing? He's praying (verse 11). Maybe he's praying something like, "Lord, here I am. I'm Your man. I'm ready to go anywhere and do anything. I want to make a difference. I want to serve You. So what's next? And oh, by the way, can You do something about my blindness?"

Well, be careful what you pray for. God answers Paul's prayer by sending a messenger who was also willing to follow God's direction. Ananias is his name, and his directions to Paul from God are rather general with no details. Speaking for God, Ananias communicates, "Paul, you are *a chosen vessel of Mine to bear My name before Gentiles, kings, and the children of Israel.* And oh, by the way, you will suffer many things for Me" (see verses 15-16).

That you pray frequently doesn't always mean you will receive quick answers. In Paul's case, more than three years went by before he was sent out from Antioch by the Holy Spirit on the first of three missionary journeys. It took that long for God's initial instructions, given by Ananias, to become a reality. Without a doubt, there were other situations throughout Paul's powerful years of ministry in which God answered some prayers immediately and not others.

## Praying for Wisdom

When we participate in prayer, we not only want to seek God's direction, we also want to seek God's wisdom when we get to our destination. And who better to give that wisdom than God, who is the source of all wisdom (Ezra 7:25)?

Are you experiencing problems or trials in your life? Are you at a crossroad in your career? Do you need wisdom for dealing with son or daughter, family member or situation, or a friend? Are you struggling through some issues in your life? If yes, what are you waiting for? God has promised you wisdom. Hear His promise:

> If any of you lacks wisdom, he should ask God,
> who gives generously to all without finding fault,
> and it will be given to him (James 1:5).

## Praying for the Right Things

Paul knew the importance of strategic prayer in his own life and the lives of others. And he knew what to pray for. His prayers focused on spiritual issues. He knew that if those he was praying for were spiritually mature, they could handle anything. We, however, sometimes have it backward. We pray about physical matters, not realizing that the real battles are fought in the spiritual realm, not the physical. That's why Paul stated that "our struggle is not against flesh and blood" (Ephesians 6:12). That's also why Paul urged believers to take up the full spiritual armor of God (verse 13). And when that's been done, Paul says to pray always...for all the saints (verse 18).

How can your prayers impact the lives of others? First, realize you may be the only one praying for a specific person. If this is the case, then your prayers to God for that individual become extremely important.

Also realize that your impact is limited only by the length of your prayer list. Just think about how many people are drawn into the plan of God as you include them in your prayers. Your life can touch and impact countless other lives when you pray. You can do what Paul did, according to Colossians 1:9-12:

Ask God to help others know what He wants them to do with their lives (verse 9).

Ask God to give others a desire for a deeper spiritual understanding (verse 9)

Ask God to help others live life in a way that pleases Him (verse 10).

Ask God to help others understand their spiritual gifts and exhibit the fruit of ministry (verse 10).

Ask God to give others strength to endure life's trials (verse 11).

Ask God to give others patience when dealing with trying people (verse 11).

Ask God to fill others with joyful thanks as they live for Him (verse 12).

Elsewhere in the New Testament we see other ways Paul prayed for people and had an influence on them:

He prayed for their purity (1 Thessalonians 5:23-24).

He prayed for righteous living that would produce fruit that would glorify God (Philippians 1:11).

He prayed that they would experience the fullness of God (Ephesians 3:18-19).

He prayed that they would be united in spirit with one another (Romans 15:5).

As you can see, there are many ways you can pray for others...and make a difference in their lives.

## Praying for God's Power

When we pray for others, we should ask God to help them grow spiritually mature. Without spiritual maturity, people will crumble at the first signs of adversity. As we just noted, Paul prayed for maturity for his friends at Colossae (1:9-12).

As we pray for the maturity of others, as Paul did, we should also pray for our own strength and power. What does Paul say this power will enable us to do? It's not the kind of power that enables you to do exceptional feats of strength. It's spiritual power that enables you to have "great endurance and patience...joyfully giving thanks to the Father" (verse 11). Your influence can't help but be felt if you have...

- the *endurance* to cope with difficult circumstances.

- the *patience* to live and function around difficult people.

- the *joy* to respond to all forms of trials with *thankfulness.*

Wow—now *that's* spiritual maturity!

## Putting God's Power to Work

So, how can you experience God's strength and power in your life? How can you become the influential man God desires for you to be? How can you realize the part you can play in fulfilling God's plan not only for you but for your family, friends, church, and—who knows— even the world? Part of the answer to these questions is found when we ask, "How can I be more faithful and consistent in my prayer life?" Start with these few suggestions for putting God's power to work in your life:

✓ *Desire to grow spiritually mature.* Maturity doesn't just happen. You must desire it and do your part. It's up to you to set a time for prayer and show up for it.

✓ *Take an honest look at your excuses for not praying.* Revisit the nine reasons we fail to pray (see pages 58-60). Identify the ones that are most obvious in your life. Then pray and ask God to help you overcome these excuses so you can become a more faithful man of prayer. Imagine how rewarding it will be when you witness God at work through your prayers!

✓ *Start a prayer list or notebook.* It doesn't have to be anything fancy. You can use a section in your daily planner or appointment book to write a list of people and things to pray for. Or you can invest in a handsome leather journal, if that will help you. You can even use something as simple as a sheet of notebook paper. Just last week a man showed me a notebook page that he uses for his prayer list. Every space on the front and back of that sheet of paper was covered with names and answers! It doesn't matter what you use—something is better that nothing. So like any businessperson, be organized as you do business with God. Then, like an accountant, be prepared to record the answers as they come!

✓ *Talk to God all through the day.* You can pray while in the car, in the shower, exercising, or running errands. Get better acquainted with God!

✓ *Set an initial goal.* Start by praying five minutes a day, or add five more minutes if you're already praying regularly. It stands to reason that the more time you spend in prayer, the more times you will "present your requests to God" (Philippians 4:6), and the more answers you will receive to your prayers.

I hope that after reading two chapters about prayer you are convinced that prayer is a vital key to having a life of impact. In fact, you will probably find yourself thinking that prayer is the *most* significant key to making a difference! Why? Because only God can answer prayer. And a prayer offered in faith and according to the will of God will marshal the power and forces of Almighty God. Now, that's impact!

> *The prayer of a righteous man*
> *is powerful and effective.*
> JAMES 5:16

*Key #3*

# Obedience

*Obedience to God's will is the*
*secret of spiritual knowledge and insight.*
*It is not willingness to know,*
*but willingness to do God's will*
*that brings certainty.*[1]

—ERIC LIDDELL

# Living a Life of Obedience

*I was not disobedient to the vision from heaven.*
—Acts 26:19

Imagine that it's sometime in the future. Life is different—*very* different! You are no longer living in a Christian-friendly society. Believers in Christ are routinely persecuted and humiliated. Christianity is under attack by the forces of evil. The Christian faith is in a fight for its life. And there you are, in your home, minding your own business, just trying to keep a low profile. You're in a comfortable chair reading a book—or your Bible—and you are contemplating how God has protected you and your family up to this point.

Suddenly a knock comes at the front door...or the phone rings. It's someone you respect very much—your pastor. And he's asking you to do the unthinkable, the impossible: to seek out the man who's responsible for much of the persecution that's taking place. You (yes, you!) are to bring that man a message from God. And, I mean, this man *hates* Christians!

Christian, whether you realize it or not, you've just come face to face with a test of your obedience to God. How will you respond?

We'll return to this scenario later. For now, though, hold on to that question while we turn our attention to another key that is necessary if you want to become a man of impact.

## To Obey or Not to Obey...

...that is the question. And every Christian must answer it, including you and me and the biblical characters whose stories follow. I have placed obedience third in our list of keys to a life of impact. Why? Unless you learn the importance of following directions from others—especially God—your life will have little to offer to others of a positive nature. We find this affirmed in the lives of some people who did obey the commands of God

*Paul*—We've already witnessed Paul's experience on the Damascus Road. But there's more! Struck blind and lying in the dirt, Paul's first words to his new Master were, "What shall I do, Lord?" (Acts 22:10). And Paul's first orders from the Master were, "Get up and go into the city, and you will be told what you must do" (Acts 9:6). Paul had a choice—to obey or not to obey. That was the question.

As we catalog the qualities that made Paul's life such a powerful instrument in the hands of God, we must quickly add obedience to that list. Obedience was a part of Paul's profile. And Paul's life was a life of power and influence because Paul's life was a life of obedience.

How long was Paul obedient to His Savior? Was it a day? A week? A month? Even a year? Answer: A man who makes a difference is a man of God whose obedience is without question, without hesitation, and at any cost...for life. Thirty years after Paul became a Christian, he boldly declared when on trial for his faith, "I was not disobedient to the vision from heaven" (Acts 26:19). In other words, from the day—even the second!—Paul experienced his miraculous supernatural encounter with Christ, he had complied with whatever God asked of him.

Now you may be thinking to yourself, *Paul's standard is too high for me. I can never be this kind of man. In fact, my life is far from where it needs to be.* Well, friend, you're not alone. I look at Paul's life and I too see how far I need to go. But you and I have to start somewhere. So let's begin by asking ourselves this simple but penetrating question:

Are there any areas of disobedience in your life that you need to deal with? If there are, I beg you to give them up! Hand them over to God. Be done with them. Get on with realizing the potential of your life as a Christian man, with living a life of influencing others.

Maybe you've had a time off, or a time out, or a time away from the Lord. Maybe your track record with God isn't as great or as smooth or as consistent as you would have liked. But don't give up. It's never too late. God's hands are always stretched out to His people (Romans 10:21), ready to help them.

*Others*—Obedience is not unique to Paul's life. The Bible contains numerous other examples of men who were asked to obey God, even in what seemed impossible circumstances. For instance,

- Abraham was asked to sacrifice his only son (Genesis 22:2)…and Abraham obeyed God.

- Moses was asked to confront Pharaoh and lead God's people out of Egypt (Exodus 3:10)…and Moses obeyed God.

- Daniel was asked to stop worshiping God or be thrown into the lion's den (Daniel 6:8-10)…and Daniel obeyed God instead.

All these men had two things in common. First, they were obedient in the midst of seemingly impossible situations. And second, their obedience equipped them to live powerful and influential lives. Just look at their impact!

- Abraham's son was spared, and Abraham was greatly blessed by God. He was known as a great leader in his day, and his descendants became the great nation of Israel. God told Abraham, "Through your offspring [Jesus] all nations on earth will be blessed," and the Bible goes on to say why: "because you have obeyed me" (Genesis 22:18).

- Moses' obedience qualified him to lead the nation of Israel out of Egypt and to the Promised Land. God gave this tribute to Moses: "My servant Moses...is faithful in all my house" (Numbers 12:7).

- Daniel was thrown into the lion's den, but God miraculously closed the mouths of the lions. Daniel's king publicly glorified God as a result of the miracle, and Daniel continued to enjoy great success as a leader (Daniel 6:28), and was called a "man of high esteem" (NASB), "greatly beloved" (NKJV) by God's messenger, Michael (Daniel 10:11). He also received numerous visions about the future because of his life of obedience.

Dear friend, each of these men was asked by God to do something. In short, Paul was asked to *get up,* Abraham was asked to *give up,* Moses was asked to *speak up,* and Daniel was asked to *stand up.* Is God asking for your obedience in any of these ways? Is He asking you to *get up* out of your La-Z-Boy chair and get more involved with your family or church? Is there something God may be asking you to *give up*—something you love that is standing between you and complete obedience and service to God? Or is there some person—or some issue—God would have you *speak up* to as a witness about the things of God? Or is there some practice in your family or at work that you should *stand up* to, or take a stand against? You and I join the ranks of the great men in the Bible when we follow God in obedience.

*Ananias*—There's one more example of obedience we simply cannot pass over. He was an ordinary person like you and me. If you're having trouble identifying with Paul, Abraham, Moses, and Daniel, this is the man for you! His is the story of a regular, insignificant (by most standards) man who was asked to do the impossible (or so it seemed!). Most people probably have not heard of him. His name was Ananias.

Ananias is a classic example of a man who displayed obedience in the midst of a difficult situation. The details of his obedience are found right in the middle of the story of Paul's conversion. In fact, Ananias's obedience was a part of that story.

Ananias was a Jewish believer who lived in Damascus. Whatever *his* reasons for being in Damascus were, God had *His* own reasons. For it was there that Ananias received the greatest test of his life...and his faith—a test not unlike the imaginary test you were given at the beginning of this chapter.

Do you remember the fictional opening story for this chapter—about bringing a message from God to a person who hates Christianity? I asked, "How would you respond?" We know how Paul, Abraham, Moses, and Daniel responded to hard situations. They obeyed! But Ananias? Let's now learn how this reluctant disciple responded.

> In Damascus there was a disciple named Ananias. The Lord called to him in a vision, "Ananias!"
>
> "Yes, Lord," he answered.
>
> The Lord told him, "Go to the house of Judas on Straight Street and ask for a man from Tarsus named Saul, for he is praying. In a vision he has seen a man named Ananias come and place his hands on him to restore his sight" (Acts 9:10-12).

Ananias did what you and I would probably have done in our imaginary situation at the beginning of this chapter—he tried to reason his way out of obedience.

*But Lord, You don't understand.*

Now listen in on the dialogue between the Lord and Ananias. Try to put yourself in Ananias's sandals.

"Lord," Ananias answered, "I have heard many reports about this man and all the harm he has done to your saints in Jerusalem. And he has come here with authority from the chief priests to arrest all who call on your name" (Acts 9:13-14).

Now, you and I know that the Lord didn't need a lecture. And He didn't need to be reminded of what kind of man Paul was. His command to Ananias was, "Go." There was no way Ananias could misinterpret the command. It was unmistakable. And Ananias had to decide—to obey, or not to obey? (There's that question again!) Would he trust the Lord? Would he obey God and go in spite of what he knew about Paul? Or would he choose to disobey the Lord?

Luke, the writer of the book of Acts, wastes no words in describing what happened next. He reports, "So Ananias departed" (Acts 9:17 NASB). And, as the saying goes, the rest is history! Humanly speaking, the obedience of this one man, Ananias, started a chain reaction of events that has marked the world and the expansion of the church to this very day. But this seemingly insignificant man's singular impact all started with his willingness to obey. His obedience made him a significant and influential force in church history.

Ananias became a man of great influence because he was obedient in the small things. His impact grew one step at a time. Here's Ananias's example to us:

- *Be available*—When the Lord called, Ananias said, "Yes, Lord."

- *Be willing*—When the Lord had finished giving Ananias His instructions, in spite of Ananias's reluctance, he departed.

- *Be prepared*—When the challenge was given, Ananias went ahead, ready to accept the consequences of his obedience. He knew Paul could mean harm to him, but he obeyed God's call to go see Paul.

- *Be expectant*—When Ananias willingly left to meet Paul, not only was Ananias prepared for the consequences, but he also went with full confidence, expecting God to work through his obedience. "Jesus…has sent me so that you may see again" (Acts 9:17).

*You*—I know we've talked a lot in this chapter about you and your obedience. And you may be thinking, *I can't measure up to people like Abraham and Paul.* But we must realize that these "heroes" of the faith were just common, ordinary people like you and me. Their obedience, however, gave these men uncommon strength for the glory of God. I don't know about you, but examples like these motivate me to re-evaluate my own obedience. Am I being asked by God to do what seems to be impossible? And because it seems to be impossible, am I wavering in the all-important area of obedience, failing to be available and willing…prepared and expectant?

## The Power of Obedience

There will never be another apostle Paul. (His exploits are many!) And leaders like Abraham, Moses, and Daniel are few and far between. But you can definitely be another Ananias. All it takes is a desire to faithfully obey the commands of Scripture as they are presented. You may be reluctant at times—as Ananias was. But if you are ultimately faithful to follow God's commands, you too can have a powerful and lasting impact on those around you.

So as a follower of Christ, the question to you is simple—*to obey… or not obey?* As we profile the lives of great people of God throughout this book, we will observe over and over again that obedience was the ingrained pattern of their life, an obvious habit that marked these men, a key that made them men who made a difference, men with a lasting impact.

Where does a life of obedience lead you? Read on in the next chapter and see how obedience can lead you down a path of joy, discovery, and impact.

*Do you know what I believe is the icing on the cake
of obedience, what I believe to be one of the most
compelling reasons for our obedience? It is this:
Obedience leads to a powerful, confident life. When
you and I are obedient, and when we allow ourselves
to be led by God through the unexpected, we then
have a confidence based on the fact that we know
we are exactly where God wants us to be. What a
joy it is to know we are at the center of God's will!*

—Jim George

# Following the Path of Obedience

*After Paul had seen the vision, we got ready at
once to leave for Macedonia, concluding that God
had called us to preach the gospel to them.*

—Acts 16:10

When my grandsons were younger, they were great fans of the children's cartoon character Bob the Builder. They had the plastic Bob the Builder hard hat, a Bob the Builder T-shirt, and a computer game in which they and Bob the Builder would build something together. For us guys, the bent toward building gets into our blood early, doesn't it? We build all kinds of things. We build houses and furniture. We also build careers, companies, and financial assets. And hopefully we are building our home life and families. Yes, we are constantly building something or hopefully building into the lives of others.

But, as we've been learning, there is something far more important for us to be concerned about building. I'm referring to building a life of influence and impact. I trust that as you've been reading along, you have been paying close attention to how obedience enables us to become men who make a difference and have a lasting impact.

So far we have seen that true impact starts by laying a firm foundation with Jesus Christ. No person's life can have a true and lasting impact without taking this essential first step. Then comes a commitment to knowing God's Word. Next, you and I need to have a viable life of prayer. Without leaving our home we can impact the lives of others through prayer. Then in the last chapter we saw that the third key to being an influence comes as we cultivate a proper spiritual life through obedience to God. With God's Word, prayer, and obedience in place, your life's structure should be taking shape. The frame for your building should be going up. But the construction process has just begun! Now let's switch metaphors and continue our travels and look at where the path of obedience leads us.

## The Path of Obedience

I'm sure by now you know what a powerful influence the life of Paul has had on me and on many others (and hopefully you, too!). I can't help but ask you to take another look at Paul's walk of obedience as we continue to determine what's involved in becoming a man who makes a difference. And I want us to pick up our journey with Paul and travel alongside him again for a time. As we fast-forward in his life, we are no longer accompanying Paul on the well-traveled Damascus Road of Syria. In fact, 20 years have passed. This time, we're going to walk beside him on a dusty back road located in what is now north-central Turkey. Paul is there because he is continuing to obey his Lord's commands to take the gospel message to the Gentiles.

Paul is now in his mid-fifties. And he's well into the second of three long and hard missionary trips. This journey will last more than three years. And Paul's obedience has not been without a price. He has been scourged countless times. He has been stoned and left for dead. He has been imprisoned in many of the towns where he has preached. Yet Paul continues to follow the path of obedience. Where does the less-traveled path of obedience lead?

To discover the exciting answers to that question I want you to do two things. First, read the Bible passage below. Then follow along with Paul through these verses to see where the path of obedience led him... and can lead you and me as well.

> Paul and his companions traveled throughout the region of Phrygia and Galatia, having been kept by the Holy Spirit from preaching the word in the province of Asia. When they came to the border of Mysia, they tried to enter Bithynia, but the Spirit of Jesus would not allow them to. So they passed by Mysia and went down to Troas. During the night Paul had a vision of a man of Macedonia standing and begging him, "Come over to Macedonia and help us." After Paul had seen the vision, we got ready at once to leave for Macedonia, concluding that God had called us to preach the gospel to them (Acts 16:6-10).

*Obedience often leads to the unexpected*—We don't know how God communicated to Paul and his missionary team. But we do know that "they were kept by the Holy Spirit from preaching the word in the province of Asia" and that "the Spirit of Jesus would not allow them" to continue to move in the direction they were traveling (verses 6-7).

As a result of God's prohibitions, Paul and his faithful companions in ministry were diverted from their intended destination in the northern region of Galatia and led instead to Troas, a city to the west. They were expecting to go north...but ended up going west.

Something similar happened to my friend Marty. (Marty, by the way, is the father-in-law of my editor and friend, Steve Miller.) Marty believed God was calling him and his family to minister in France. Therefore he started language training and prepared to go to France. But God had other plans. Marty was expecting to minister in France, but he ended up using his French to minister to the people of Montreal, Canada. As Marty was obedient to God, he experienced the unexpected.

How about you? Are you fearful because God is moving you in an unexpected direction? Is the unknown causing you to waver on the path of obedience? Take heart in your resolve. Walk in confidence with God. Walk as King David did, declaring, "Even though I walk through the valley of the shadow of death, I will fear no evil, for you are with me" (Psalm 23:4).

Like Paul and his team, you and I don't always know where God's will may take us. Oh, we may think we do! But often our obedience will lead us to the unexpected. And that's okay, for that's exactly where God wants us. *Often the center of God's will lies in the unexpected.*

*Obedience often leads to clarification*—As Paul and his men chose to continue to obey God's leading, God's will and direction for their lives became clearer and clearer. It was as if God was saying, "Hey, no, guys! It's not *that* direction...it's *this* direction!" The missionaries thought they were to evangelize the northern cities of Asia Minor. But with obedience came clear direction to leave Asia and to instead witness to the people of Macedonia (known today as Greece), a totally different region off to the west.

If Paul and his men had stopped at any point along the way, they might not have fully realized God's complete plan for their lives and ministry. Think again of my friend Marty. As Marty continued to follow the Lord's direction, his ministry destination was further clarified. What an influence Marty and his family had upon the people of Montreal! Why? Because Marty continued to heed God's direction, allowing God to work and to reveal His will at the right time.

I've had this happen in my own life as well. After our family returned from a time of missionary service in Singapore, I was at a crossroad. I thought I was to seek a pulpit ministry. So I applied for numerous pastoral positions. However, I was always the second-favorite candidate. I was getting pretty frustrated. I thought this was what God was calling me to, so why was this happening over and over again? Then one day, in the midst of my frustration (or should I say my lack of trust?), I was asked to join the faculty at Talbot School of Theology in Southern California.

Looking back, I can see how God was directing me through "closed" and "open" doors. He had a purpose for me at Talbot, and that led to other things. Even now I can see God continuing to clarify the direction of my life as I am obedient to follow His will. And much to my surprise, His power is always most evident when I willingly and obediently allow Him to make clear the path before me.

Are you beginning to see why obedience is such an important part of living a life of impact? You and I will never fully know the will of God and the power of God in our lives without obedience. *Obedience clarifies God's will.*

*Obedience leads us as we listen*—During the formative years of Christianity, before the New Testament was in written form, Jesus often communicated with the fledgling church through visions and dreams. We've already witnessed this in God's guidance of Paul and Ananias, as mentioned in earlier chapters, and now here it is again. The Bible doesn't say how God communicated with Paul and his team, whether by visions, dreams, or a voice, or even by a prophet like Agabus (Acts 11:27-28). But we do know Paul and his crew were sensitive to the Spirit's leading and they listened to God obediently. They desired God's will and looked for it. And when it came, they listened. As a result, they were led by God until they ended up with God's final directive—a vision of a man from the region of Macedonia begging them to come there.

This is an obvious lesson for you and me as well. Are you sensitive to God's leading? The real test of your sensitivity comes with what follows!

## The Provisions for Obedience

This, of course, raises an important question: How does God communicate to His people today? It's not that God couldn't speak to you in a vision or a dream. Rather, it's that today, He speaks through what I call "the four C's":

C-ommands from the inspired Word of God

C-ompetent and wise counselors

C-ircumstances and changing conditions

C-onscience aided by the Holy Spirit

Friend, at one time or another, God will use any or all of these means to give direction to you if you are ready to listen. In my case, God used the wise counsel of my pastor and guidance from some close friends as I struggled with whether to continue pursuing a pulpit ministry or to accept a seminary teaching position.

Whether you are a pastor, a plumber, a painter, an office worker, young or old, a Paul or a new Christian, you need to ask yourself: Am I listening as God speaks to me through some or all of these means? You will never know the will of God if you are not sensitive to God's Spirit and therefore tune out His voice, which may come through any of these different avenues. How can I say this with such certainty? Because…

- You can never obey a command that you never read in the Bible.

- You can never obey godly advice that you never ask for or accept.

- You can never obey God's leading through circumstances and changes if you are not willing to obey in the midst of those circumstances and changes.

- You can never obey the Spirit's leading if you are not listening with a heart that's willing to obey.

Obedience to the will of God is possible only as we listen when God speaks to us through any of these four means of communication. *Are you listening?*

*Obedience leads us one decision at a time*—Question: How did Paul get to the point in his life where he was looking across the Aegean Sea toward a new mission field? Answer: He arrived at it…one act of obedience at a time. Paul's path of obedience started on the Damascus Road. But it didn't stop there. As soon as Paul could see…he was obedient to be baptized. And it didn't stop there. As soon as he regained his strength…he began to preach. And it didn't stop there. It continued on, one step at a time…until Paul could reflect back on more than 25 years as a Christian and state before kings, "I was not disobedient to the vision" (Acts 26:19).

Dear brother, your impact on the lives of others—your family, the people at your church, your workmates—is cultivated with each life-decision you make. It's the little things—such as reading your Bible, praying, going to church, and standing up for your faith at work—that add influence to your life. Obey God one decision at a time and see where it leads you. Always remember: *The key to a powerful Christian life is obedience to our Lord's leading—one decision at a time.*

*Obedience leads to confident living*—As we've already seen, Paul and Company finally made it to Troas, where they received the vision of the man from Macedonia. Then these words—"we got ready *at once* to leave for Macedonia"—were used to describe the group's eagerness to obey God's leading once they understood the command (Acts 16:10). (Don't fail to notice their teachable spirit…as well as their *confident* spirit!)

Now comes the icing on the cake—what I believe to be one of the most compelling reasons for our obedience. It is this: Obedience leads to a powerful, confident life. After Paul and his team had seen the vision, they got ready at once to leave for Macedonia, *concluding that God had called them to preach the gospel there* (verse 10). Can't you just feel the confidence these men had as they now knew what God wanted them to do?

When you and I are obedient, and when we allow ourselves to be led by God through the unexpected, we then have a confidence based on the fact that we know we are exactly where God wants us to be. What a joy it is to know we are at the center of God's will! Then we, along with Paul, can confidently lead and boldly influence others as we declare, "Follow my example, as I follow the example of Christ" (1 Co-rinthians 11:1). Indeed, *obedience leads to a powerful, confident life.*

## A Desire to Be Obedient

Now, how about you? Wouldn't you like to have that kind of con-fidence in your life? Wouldn't you like to live a powerful and influen-tial life? Wouldn't you like your life to have a lasting impact and give glory to God?

If your answer is yes (and I can't imagine why it wouldn't be!), then ask God to give you the strength to obey His commands as they come to you. And how will God's commands come? They will come…

> …as you faithfully read His Word,
>
> …as you faithfully hear the preaching of His Word,
>
> …as you faithfully listen to wise counsel from His Word, and
>
> …as you faithfully deal with sin in your life as revealed by the piercing light of His Word.

A desire to obediently follow the Lord's leading *should* be the supreme goal of your life. Is it? Your willingness to trust and obey the Lord is a key step toward experiencing God's blessings in your life. And it is a key element in becoming a man who makes a difference.

With that in mind, let *your* heart sing the words of the beloved, time-honored hymn of commitment to obedience that appears on the next page.

### *Trust and Obey*

When we walk with the Lord
in the light of His Word,
What a glory He sheds on our way!
While we do His good will
He abides with us still,
And with all who will trust and obey.
Trust and obey,
For there's no other way
To be happy in Jesus,
But to trust and obey.[1]

*Key #4*

# Challenges

*A university professor noticed a student was about to fall asleep in class. So the teacher asked the student, "What is the greatest problem in our society— ignorance or apathy?" The student replied, "I don't know and I don't care."*[1]

# Mastering Life's Challenges

*Judge for yourselves whether it is right in God's
sight to obey you rather than God.*

—Acts 4:19

❧

As a boy growing up in Oklahoma, I, like most of my friends, loved
football. I even tried out for my local high school squad. Well,
my lessons in humility began right then and there—I was cut before
the end of the first week of tryouts!

Not wanting to give up on my athletic aspirations, I next tried running the hurdles on the track team. Timing was everything. To clear
each hurdle, I had to run as hard as I could for an exact number of
steps, then jump…and hope to clear the hurdle. I have to report (with
even more humility) that the challenge of the hurdles was too much
for me. I settled for running the half-mile and the mile (and still run
to this day).

My brief attempt at jumping hurdles is a good illustration of what can happen as we seek to commit ourselves to a life of obedience. We *want* to obey God…but along comes a hurdle. At that point, we have a choice: We can decide it's not worth the effort and give up, or we can continue down the path of obedience and learn the secret of doing what it requires to master and take the hurdles one by one as they come. That brings us to our fourth key: We must learn to master the challenges, the hurdles, that are certain to arise in our attempt to live a life of impact.

## The Church Began with Challenges

To begin, realize you and I are in good company! From the very beginning of the church, the early disciples faced challenges. Their first challenge was to choose whether they would serve the risen Christ or bow to the pressures of the religious leaders of their day. Even before Paul's relentless persecution of the church, Peter and John, two of Jesus' 12 disciples, were called before the Sanhedrin, the main religious counsel in Israel. There, they were seriously threatened and commanded to stop preaching in the name of Jesus.

What happened? These men of God—and men whose influence for Christ has reached across the past 2000 years—resisted. How? They courageously declared, "Judge for yourselves whether it is right in God's sight to obey you rather than God. For we cannot help speaking about what we have seen and heard" (Acts 4:19-20).

The path of obedience is seldom easy. And it wasn't easy for the first disciples in the church. But the faithful band of early believers resisted the challenge to disobey their risen Savior's command to be His witnesses (Acts 1:8).

And what was the effect of their obedience? "They were all filled with the Holy Spirit and spoke the word of God boldly" (Acts 4:31). Their obedience was fueled by the power of the Holy Spirit, and their influence was felt even to the ends of the earth (Acts 1:8). Now *that's* influence! May you and I courageously master the challenges that come our way and follow the pattern of obedience set by these men of old!

This seems like a good place to pause and ask, Who are you serving, my friend? The risen Savior, or someone (or something) else? Are you making an effort to clear the hurdles before you? Are you standing firm in obedience? And are you standing up for your Christian beliefs? Jesus Christ was the beginning of the church, and He is the beginning (and the end!) of the life of every man of influence. To have a lasting impact for Christ and to leave an indelible mark on this world, you too must obey Christ and master the challenges.

## The Challenges of Obedience

As we've already seen, obedience wasn't easy for Paul and his men. Paul's path was riddled with challenges. He and his team of missionaries had (and would!) face many challenges to their faith. No, obedience is never easy. In fact, it's downright hard! But obedience is what God asked of Paul and his men. And obedience was what God asked of the early disciples. And, my friend, if we are to have an impact, obedience is what God is asking of us—even with all its challenges.

Obedience to God always has its challenges. Maybe this is why it's the less-traveled path. Disobedience, on the other hand, seems to be the more traveled, more well-worn path. In fact, it is characterized by gridlock! Why? Because disobedience is the easy path. It's the path we're tempted to take when things get sticky. It's the path with the least challenges. And sadly, it's the path that makes us men of little or no positive impact.

What are some of the challenges that we face in our quest to be a man who makes a difference? As we run the race for Christ, what are the hurdles that trip us up, knock us down, or pressure us to compromise and rationalize what we know to be God's standards? And how can you and I overcome and master these challenges and keep moving onward in our desire to become men who make a difference?

I'm sure you probably have a few "pet" challenges in your own life. As I share a few of mine—a few that have bothered and derailed my life over the years—you will probably find yourself thinking of some of your own challenges.

*The challenge of ignorance*—One of the most tragic challenges to obedience and godly influence is ignorance—about the commands of Scripture. We live in a day and age of biblical illiteracy. Christians, I'm sad to say, are increasingly ignorant of spiritual truths. Knowing God's Word just doesn't seem to have the priority it used to have. Maybe it's their hectic lifestyles that keep them too preoccupied to spend time in God's Word. Christians don't know what the Bible has to say about the issues and struggles they face every day. Such ignorance causes us to fail to live boldly for Christ.

And ignorance of any kind costs us, too—I know! I know it from an experience I had several years ago: One day when I was driving only 35 miles an hour, I was pulled over by a policeman for speeding. I tried to explain to the officer that I hadn't seen the sign that read "School Zone—20 Miles Per Hour." How far did my plea of ignorance get me with that officer? You guessed it—a $120 fine!

God, too, has a standard of conduct for His people. And brother, the Bible details that standard. On at least four occasions Paul begged his readers to not be *ignorant* of God's plans.[2] Let's heed Paul's admonition…and his heart. He pleaded, "I do not want you to be *ignorant*" (Romans 11:25). In other words, Paul (like the police officer) is saying ignorance is no excuse.

Having taught at a seminary for so many years, I can't resist taking a moment to give you a quick pop quiz!

- On a scale of 1 to 10, how would you rate your knowledge of God's Word?
- On a scale of 1 to 10, how would you rate your knowledge of your favorite sports team, the latest food recipes, or the stars of your favorite TV shows?
- Which gets the higher rating—your sports team, the recipes, the TV stars, or God's Word?

Maybe you're not into sports, recipes, or television. Then I invite you to rate your knowledge of God's Word against whatever it is that can easily divert your attention. Then ask yourself the same question: Which gets the higher score?

Are you getting the picture? Your Christian influence comes from the power of God's Word, not from your knowledge of the things of this world. If you want to be a man who makes a difference, you cannot be ignorant of the Bible's teachings. As D.L. Moody, preacher-of-old and influencer-of-many, put it, "I never met a useful Christian who was not a student of the Bible."[3]

*The challenge of the flesh*—Every Christian would agree that the presence of sin in our world is a fact of life that challenges our obedience. From the second that sin entered the world through Adam and Eve's disobedience, all mankind (including you and me) entered into a struggle with obedience. Sometimes that struggle is with God and His Word. Sometimes it's with governmental authority and laws—laws like speed limits, our bosses, or our own conscience.

Friend, *every* Christian man battles with the flesh...even the great apostle Paul struggled. As you read below from the book of Romans, sense the conflict between Paul's sinful flesh and his desire to obey God. (And take note that Paul was in his late fifties when he wrote these words. Mastering the flesh is a lifelong battle!) But don't miss the victory. There is hope for us!

> So I find this law at work: When I want to do good, evil is right there with me. For in my inner being I delight in God's law; but I see another law at work in the members of my body, waging war against the law of my mind and making me a prisoner of the law of sin at work within my members. What a wretched man I am! Who will rescue me from this body of death? Thanks be to God—through Jesus Christ our Lord! (Romans 7:21-24).

Yes, the battles of the flesh are real. But you can master your flesh—rather than letting it master you. Here are some practical steps to M-A-S-T-E-R the challenges of the flesh.

**M**-onitor your time with those who drag you down, whether they be friends, workmates, or family.

**A**-ccount for your struggles to a more spiritually mature Christian.

**S**-trengthen your inner man by the study of God's Word and through prayer.

**T**-rain your eyes to avoid anything that might fan the flames of your fleshly desires.

**E**-xercise purity in all your relationships with the opposite sex.

**R**-un from the lusts of the flesh.

*The challenge of apathy*—Ignorance breeds apathy. And apathy for a Christian—a Christian meant to live boldly for Christ—is like dying of hypothermia, like freezing to death. When you and I are exposed too long to the cold winds of ignorance and compromise, we slowly drift through complacency into the icy death of apathy. The book of Revelation describes this drift into apathy as being "lukewarm—neither hot nor cold" (Revelation 3:16).

Apathy is not just a modern-day spiritual challenge. (Just read the book of Judges, where the people of Israel struggled repeatedly with complacency!) Given the distractions and temptations all around us, it's easy for us to flirt with apathy. We go our own way. We become cold and hardened to the ways of God. We begin to live our life as "practical atheists." We start living as if there is no God (or at least a God we are accountable to). Then, one day, surprise of surprises(!), we get into trouble…and *then* we cry out to God to bail us out. Suddenly we are eager to obey God's commands, but not until our apathy has led us down the path of disobedience and its resultant pain and consequences.

Apathy is such a subtle challenge. In fact, it is so subtle that I didn't even see it coming until it was too late. Let me explain. I went away to college to study to become a pharmacist. I fully intended to continue my habit of going to church and being active in student ministry.

However, little by little I stopped going to church on a regular basis. I was too busy with college life and my studies to be involved with other Christians at church activities. Eventually I got to the point where I was "spiritually frozen." For the next ten years I was in the grips of spiritual apathy. I was useless to God. I was barren of any spiritual life and fruit. I was even having a *negative* influence on others because of my apathy.

It's sobering, isn't it? You and I better believe it—apathy is deadly! And none of us is immune to it. I wasn't, and you aren't immune to its icy touch either. I hope you never end up at the same point I reached. How did I survive apathy? It was the grace of God that came to my aid.

Friend, apathy is a heart condition. It turns your heart for God into a heart that thinks it can exist without God. How do you keep from drifting into spiritual apathy? How can you keep apathy from settling into your life? Check your spiritual temperature on a regular basis by asking these questions:

> Am I making excuses for missing church?
>
> Am I becoming comfortable with little sins?
>
> Am I able to take or leave God's Word?
>
> Am I spending more of my discretionary hours with non-Christians rather than Christians?
>
> Am I looking to myself or the world rather than to God for help with life issues?
>
> Am I resisting the warnings of fellow believers?

If your answer to any or most of these questions is *yes,* then, my brother, you are well on your way to apathy. But realize that with God's help, you can overcome the problem. Speaking as a former pharmacist, here is my "spiritual prescription" for dealing with apathy.

℞   Recognize that apathy can happen to you.

℞   Realize that God's Word is essential.

℞   Reach out to those with "hot hearts" for the Lord.

℞  Regularly attend church.

℞  Request that others hold you accountable for your commitments to God.

## The Keys to Mastering Life's Challenges

Ignorance, the flesh, and apathy—these are three definite challenges that can cause Christians to stumble on the path to becoming a person of influence. But the three keys to mastering these three challenges are:

- acknowledging the challenges of ignorance, the flesh, and apathy,
- looking to God for help, and
- taking appropriate action.

Friend, do you see it? Ultimately it's *you* who determines whether you want to remain ignorant of God's Word. It's *you* who decides whether you want to give in to the flesh. It's *you* who dictates whether you drift into apathy. All three of these challenges can be mastered as *you* look to God for His strength in the inner man.

*A person who can master the challenges of
the inner life will unquestionably have
an influence on others.*

Now that we are alert to the challenges that can come from *within* us, stay with me as we move on to the next chapter and look at some of the challenges that face us from *without.*

*It is only the fear of God that can
deliver us from the fear of man.*[1]

—JOHN WITHERSPOON

# Accepting the Challenge to Live Boldly

*Be strong in the Lord, and in the strength of His might.*

—EPHESIANS 6:10 (NASB)

Have you ever tried to define *obedience*? That's the challenge a missionary ran up against as he was translating the Bible. Taking a break from his search for a meaning, he called to his dog. When the dog came running, a tribal observer said, "Your dog was all ear." Instantly the missionary had the words he needed to define *obedience*—"to be all ear."

I'm sure by now you've noticed obedience is a key element in becoming a man who makes a difference. And, in the previous chapter, we learned about the challenges that make obedience difficult—the challenges of ignorance, the flesh, and apathy. Let's continue on with our list of challenges that a Christian man faces every day. And as we do so, let's aim at accepting God's challenge to live in *bold* obedience—to be all ear!

## The Challenges of Obedience

*The challenge of fear*—One of the biggest challenges you and I face in our obedience to God is the fear of reprisal—fear of the consequences of doing the right thing. Ananias was afraid of what Paul had done to Christians and of what Paul might do to him. Ananias's fear tempted him to waver in his obedience to God's desire to use him as a man of influence and impact.

The challenge of this type of fear is not limited to Ananias or you or me. (And don't say you are never challenged with fear!) Even the great apostle Paul had his bouts with fear. For instance, Paul's path of obedience to God ultimately led him through Macedonia to the great cities of Athens and Corinth (Acts 17–18). Both of these cities were very large...and very decadent.

Corinth was especially worldly and immoral. This great city housed the temple of Aphrodite, the goddess of love, with its 1000 priestess-prostitutes. In the ancient world of Paul's day, Corinth was noted for everything sinful. Referring back to his initial visit to this corrupt city, Paul later wrote to the Corinthians that his exposure to them and their city was "in weakness and *fear,* and with much trembling" (1 Corinthians 2:3). All men of influence experience fear at some time or other. And here's another fact: Fear usually comes when we are in a hostile environment and must stand up for our faith.

While you and I are not being asked to walk into a sinful place like Corinth, we *are* being asked to stand up and speak up for the Christian faith and Christian values in the midst of an antagonistic workplace or at our child's school. We are confronted with the sinfulness of our society not on an irregular basis, but daily! And if you're anything like me, you are not immune to fear when those situations occur.

But the issue is not our fear. Fear is normal. No, the issue is our *response* to fear. Fear can either immobilize us or be used as a bridge to power—God's power that can work in us. Paul explains from his own life how he asked the Lord three times to take away a mysterious "thorn in my flesh." And what was God's answer? "My grace is sufficient for you, for my power is made perfect in weakness" (2 Corinthians 12:8). God empowered Paul in his fears and weaknesses to face the challenges in his life.

The next time you should stand up for Christ and fear starts welling up, you need to first recognize you're too weak to handle the situation alone. Then you need to pray that God would override your fears so that whenever you open your mouth, words may be given to you so you "will *fearlessly* make known the mystery of the gospel" (Ephesians 6:19).

*The challenge of peer pressure*—Peer pressure is the twin sister of fear. Peer pressure creates a fear not of our enemies and hostile situations, but of our family, friends, workmates, and neighbors—our peers. We're afraid that others will laugh at us, or reject us, or torment us if we stand up for our faith and God's standards.

If you think you're the only one who has struggled with this challenge, think again. Read below how peer pressure in all its power affected the great apostle Peter and even Paul's close friend Barnabas. Paul reports,

> When Peter came to Antioch, I opposed him to his face, because he was clearly in the wrong. Before certain men came from James, he used to eat with the Gentiles. But when they arrived, he began to draw back and separate himself from the Gentiles because he was *afraid* of those who belonged to the circumcision group. The other Jews joined him in his hypocrisy, so that by their hypocrisy even Barnabas was led astray (Galatians 2:11-13).

In short, these two men—men who were supposed to be men of influence—had caved in to peer pressure.

Does this sound familiar? I know it does for me. I've caved in at one time or another when I allowed peer pressure to overrule what I knew to be God's standard. And I'm sure you're aware that every day you must decide, *Will I follow the crowd, or will I boldly follow Christ?* You cannot follow both! So…which will it be?

Again, let's take Paul's cue on boldness in the face of peer pressure. What did he do? Paul requested that others pray for him so that whenever he opened his mouth, "words may be given me so that I will *fearlessly* make known the mystery of the gospel" (Ephesians 6:19).

Like Paul, be B-O-L-D.

> **B**-e not afraid.
>
> **O**-btain the prayer support of others.
>
> **L**-ook to the Lord for His strength.
>
> **D**-ecide daily to boldly follow Christ.

*The challenge of our culture*—Living a bold and godly life in an ungodly culture is also a constant challenge. Any time you stand up for what you believe, you will be challenged by your culture—you can count on it! As Paul told his young disciple, Timothy, "*Everyone* who wants to live a godly life in Christ Jesus will be persecuted" (2 Timothy 3:12). Fellow Christian man, when you signed on as a soldier of Jesus Christ, you signed on to a life that is not to be "entangled with the affairs of everyday life" (2 Timothy 2:3 NASB). You *live* in this world, but you are not to *love* this world (1 John 2:15). Just because some people cheat on their taxes or pad their expense accounts or make shady deals—and just because such acts seem to be culturally accepted—doesn't make it okay for you to do such things. No, you are to live boldly by different standards—God's standards!

Several years ago I came up against this challenge of culture. I was trying to sell a used boat trailer in the middle of winter. (Do you know how hard it is to sell a boat trailer when it's hardly 30 degrees outside and no one is boating?) Well, you can imagine how thankful I was to the Lord when a potential buyer contacted me. This man was even willing to pay my asking price. The only catch was that he wanted me to put only half the worth of the trailer on the bill of sale. He said, "That's the way we do it in these parts." If I complied, he wouldn't have to pay but half the state sales tax, which amounted to several hundred dollars. I have to confess that my first thoughts were along these lines: *I really want to sell that trailer…but if I say no, he might back out…and I may not be able to find anyone else who will pay my asking price…but if I agree, then I will be lying (not to mention breaking the law!)…but who would know…?*

There I was, for the first few moments having this inner struggle, thinking all these terrible thoughts, knowing all the time what I should do, but still struggling! Well, brother, you will be glad to know that I refused his illicit offer. In fact, I told him boldly I was a Christian and that I didn't want to do anything illegal. I wanted to be obedient to God's standards, and I was prepared to lose the sale rather than go along with what was culturally acceptable in "these parts." (And, by the way, the man did pay me the full price, and I did declare the full amount on the bill of sale.)

While I didn't lose the sale, I was prepared to do so. And there will be times when you and I will "lose out" because we won't compromise. But, believe me, that "loss" is nothing compared to what is gained— God's blessing for our obedience, and a clear conscience for doing what is right.

Friend, you are called to live boldly and obediently by different standards—God's standards. That means you must…

- Find out God's standards.
- Make God's standards your standards.
- Determine to live by those standards.
- Be willing to accept the consequences of living by those standards.
- Be accountable to others for following God's standards.
- Pray for God's strength to help you boldly withstand the pressures to compromise God's standards.

## Accepting the Challenges

I'm not much of a student of the laws of physics, but it doesn't take much of a student to understand that where there is no resistance, there is no pressure. And that same law could apply to our spiritual lives as well—where there is no resistance to sin (that is, when we disobey), there is no challenge to obedience. There are no challenges...

...when you allow fear to immobilize you

...when you allow peer pressure to compromise you

...when you allow your culture to conform you

...when you allow ignorance to stupefy you

...when you allow apathy to pacify you

But I think better of you. I believe you are ready to accept the challenges that come with obedience. I believe you want your life to have a bold impact for God...and that you want to become a man of godly influence. With God's help (and that's what it will take) you are ready to be used in powerful ways by God.

Here then are a few suggestions that will definitely help you develop a life of influence and lasting impact. And forgive me if I repeat myself, but you and I can never be reminded enough of these simple steps!

Step 1: *Realize that God's Word is God's Word to you.* As an excuse for disobedience, some people say, "If God would speak to me in a vision like He did to Paul and Ananias, or like He did with Moses, then I would obey." But friend, God *has* revealed Himself to us! God has revealed Himself to us in His Son, Jesus Christ, and in His Word, the Bible. Let's stop making excuses and start obeying God's Word.

Step 2: *Realize what God's commands are and obey them.*
What kind of commands? Commands like...

- "Husbands, love your wives" (Ephesians 5:25).
- "Whatever you do, work at it with all your heart, as working for the Lord, not for men" (Colossians 3:23).

- "Everyone must submit himself to the governing authorities" (Romans 13:1).

- "Each of you must put off falsehood and speak truthfully" (Ephesians 4:25).

- "Go and make disciples of all nations" (Matthew 28:19).

*Step 3: Constantly seek God's strength to follow through on His commands.* "Be strong in the Lord and in the strength of His might" (Ephesians 6:10 NASB). What God *expects* you to do, He also *enables* you to do. The strength comes from Him. You just need a willing heart.

*Step 4: Repent when you have disobeyed God's standards.* God is not asking you to be perfect, but He *is* asking you to progress and grow in maturity. God uses pure vessels. So...

...keep a clean slate with God,

...acknowledge your sin,

...accept the forgiveness God offers, and

...move on boldly for God.

*Step 5: Rejoice in even the smallest victories.* No war is ever won in one battle. And neither is your war against the challenge to obedience. Spiritual growth happens one step at a time, one victory at a time. So thank God even for the smallest of victories in Jesus Christ (Romans 7:24).

> Your outcome in life
> doesn't depend on your income,
> but on how you overcome.

As I've said before, it all comes down to this: *An influential life* for *God is dependent on an obedient life* to *God.*

*Key #5*

# Discipline

*We will never get anywhere in life*
*without discipline…*
*This is doubly so in spiritual matters.*
*None of us naturally seeks after God…*
*As children of grace, our spiritual*
*discipline is everything—everything!*
*I repeat…discipline is everything![1]*

# Pursuing Spiritual Discipline

*Train yourself to be godly.*
—1 Timothy 4:7

✣

I'm sure you've heard and probably read many inspiring stories about those who have overcome great adversity and overwhelming odds to compete in the Olympics or some other world-class sports event. One such story that has inspired and challenged me is that of Lance Armstrong.

Lance won seven consecutive first-place finishes from 1999–2005 in the grueling 2000-mile, three-week long Tour de France, the premiere event in cycling. What makes Lance's story so amazing is that he won his first title less than three years after being diagnosed with an advanced form of cancer that had spread to his lungs and brain. He was given a 40-percent chance of survival and underwent brain surgery and chemotherapy.

The very nature of Lance Armstrong's accomplishments has made him a man of influence. His life shows us what the human spirit can achieve with discipline, determination, and mental toughness (along with good doctors and the latest medicines). Lance is a world-class cyclist, and to reach this level of impact he has had to exert super-human effort just to prepare himself to compete, not to mention to win in competition! His persistent life of rigorous training illustrates yet another of the keys to a life of lasting impact—discipline.

## The Focus on Discipline

As we have already witnessed, one man of major-league influence was the apostle Paul. And one of the reasons for Paul's great impact on others was that he was a disciplined man! There's no doubt about it. Like our cycling friend Lance Armstrong, Paul was a competitor and highly motivated. Where, we might wonder, did he get his drive? Was it because of his strict religious training as a Pharisee? Was it what some people call a type A personality?

These elements may have contributed to Paul's drive, but the real reason for Paul's discipline was the focus of his life. Paul passionately and persistently focused on the "crown that will last forever" (1 Corinthians 9:25). Lance Armstrong, and others who compete at any level in any sports event or business venture, have their earthly reasons for their high levels of motivation—an earthly prize, a "crown that will not last." But Paul's motivation was Jesus Christ—an eternal prize. And brother, that focus made all the difference! Paul wanted to *pursue* the knowledge of Jesus Christ (Philippians 3:10). Paul wanted to *preach* the message of Jesus Christ (1 Corinthians 9:16). And Paul was willing to *pay any price* and do whatever it took to stay in the Christian race for Jesus Christ. As I said, Jesus Christ was the complete focus of Paul's life. And the more Jesus Christ influenced Paul, the more Paul influenced others.

### Your Personal Passion

Paul's motivation to please Jesus Christ and to obtain an eternal prize were chief contributors to his life of discipline. These were his goals and his passion. And friend, like Paul, you and I have certain people or things who are driving our life. So I ask you, What is motivating you these days? What is getting you up early every morning and keeping you up late at night? What is consuming the hours and days of your life? Is it a career? Is it a desire for success? Is it the goal of financial independence? Is it a dream of future happiness or retirement?

These desires in and of themselves may not be wrong or evil. But what happens when you reach any of these physical or financial goals, these "earthly" prizes? Will you be satisfied? Maybe. But also maybe not. My friend, here's the hard question: Are you willing to take a chance and expend your life and energies on these kinds of pursuits that, in the end, might *not* fulfill your deepest longings? While you're thinking about your answer, read on.

### Paul's Personal Passion

I hope you're learning a lot about the apostle Paul. This man's life-study has become a passionate lifetime pursuit for me. And now we're going to look at yet another way he can school us toward becoming men who make a difference.

Paul was a man who had it all. He had the right background, the right job, and was the best at what he did. He was making excellent progress toward the top of his "profession." But after he became a Christian, Paul saw his accomplishments and goals in a different light. So he gave up all his earthly and personal pursuits for something better—far better! He gave all of it up for a life of following hard after Jesus Christ. Hear the heart of Paul as he searches for the words to describe for us the new focus of his life:

> Whatever was to my profit I now consider loss for the sake of Christ. What is more, I consider everything a loss compared to the surpassing greatness of knowing Christ Jesus my Lord, for whose sake I have lost all things. I consider them rubbish, that I may gain Christ (Philippians 3:7-8).

My friend, discipline is a good and profitable thing. You will never get anywhere without it. You will never be a man of influence on any level without discipline. But make sure your discipline has the right focus, the right direction. Like Paul, make sure your goal is, first and foremost, Jesus Christ. Then all else will fall into place. In fact, that's what Jesus Himself said: "Seek first the kingdom of God and His righteousness and all these things [the necessities of life] shall be added to you" (Matthew 6:33 NKJV).

As you can see from Christ's words, discipline for the Christian man is really *spiritual* discipline. As we put our time and energy into our spiritual life, God replaces old destructive habits and thoughts with godly habits and God-honoring thoughts and desires.

Lance Armstrong and others like him most definitely have positions of influence in life and society, and we want to acknowledge their noteworthy accomplishments and learn from them. But true and lasting impact comes from living our lives for Jesus Christ, as Paul discovered. Such a God-honoring life has the greatest kind of impact on others. *That is why pursuing spiritual discipline is the next key to a life of impact.* Therefore, if we want to be men who make a difference—and we do—then we have to ask the obvious question: How do we get this kind of life? This is where spiritual discipline comes in.

## The Characteristics of Spiritual Discipline

Paul gives us a simple description of spiritual discipline in a letter to his young disciple Timothy: *Train yourself to be godly.* From this simple-but-profound admonition to Timothy (found in 1 Timothy 4:7) we can discern three characteristics of spiritual discipline.

1. *Spiritual discipline is demanding*—"*Train* yourself to be godly." This act of "training" is also translated "discipline" (NASB) and "exercise" (KJV), issuing to us the command to constantly discipline ourselves to be godly. The word "train" speaks of the rigorous, strenuous, self-sacrificing training a good athlete undergoes.[2] Therefore, my friend, Paul is urging you, as he urged his protégé Timothy, to continually and

rigorously pursue a life of godly discipline. And, just as an athlete cannot afford to take a day off in his physical training without suffering a physical setback, neither can you or I afford to take time off from our spiritual discipline…even though the cost of spiritual discipline is great and very demanding.

I have experienced two vocational moves in my life. The first involved moving out of the pharmaceutical profession and into full-time ministry. As you might imagine, my spiritual growth was greatly accelerated by my involvement in ministry and the time such ministry requires in spiritual pursuits and preparations. The second move came several years ago when I moved out of "professional ministry" and into a writing and speaking ministry. With the second move I incorrectly assumed that because I was researching and writing and speaking about spiritual things, I didn't need to spend as much of my personal time pursuing spiritual disciplines such as reading my Bible and praying.

Things were fine for a while…until I, along with my wife, began to notice some ungodly behavior beginning to creep in—behavior such as impatience, irritability, and even hints of anger. The changes were so subtle! And all due to a seemingly small thing, like failing to read my Bible regularly for my own spiritual growth. But the cost to my spiritual life was great! Friend, take it from me: Spiritual discipline is demanding, and must be a constant pursuit!

2. *Spiritual discipline must be desired*—Look at Paul's words again. But this time, catch a different message as you focus on a different word. He said, "Train *yourself* to be godly." Brother, this is not a suggestion! Godliness is not optional. No, God desires that you and I, as His men, along with Paul and Timothy, be conformed to the image of His Son (Romans 8:29). This desire must be at the very heart of our being. This hunger for self-disciplined training in the ways of God must go beyond the wishing stage and become reality as we actually do something about spiritual discipline.

I don't know about you, but I know that if I want to stay healthy, I should do something about my body every day. I need to participate in some form of physical exercise. My head says yes, but my heart and body say no. (And you can guess which part of me usually wins!) Well, this same scenario plays out in the spiritual realm. My heart says yes, but my flesh says, *Let's do something spiritual some other time.*

The truth is that in both the physical and the spiritual realms of a man's life, the only way to make the "workout" a reality is by an act of the will. Ultimately, I have to decide to get up from my couch and go do some physical exercise. And the same is required in my spiritual life. Ultimately, I have to decide to get up from my couch and go get my Bible.

So how can you move forward on your desire to become a man who makes a difference? Answer: Ask God to give you a greater desire to grow spiritually. (And while you're at it, ask Him to help you get up off *your* couch and do something physical as well!)

3. *Spiritual discipline points toward God*—Once again, let's consider Paul's words to Timothy (and us), but this time with a different emphasis: "Train yourself *to be godly.*" *Godliness* is at the center of the Christian life. Therefore, godliness should be the direction of every believer's life. What is godliness? I believe this definition goes straight to the heart of what it means:

> Godliness is a right attitude and response toward the true
> Creator God; a preoccupation from the heart with holy
> and sacred realities. It is respect for what is due to God,
> and is thus the highest of all virtues.[3]

If you and I are God's children, then we should want to be like God as much as is humanly possible. But our sinful flesh resists this goal. Even the great apostle Paul struggled in this area. Hear again...and sense again...his constant battle:

> So I find this law at work: When I want to do good, evil
> is right there with me. For in my inner being I delight in
> God's law; but I see another law at work in the members

of my body, waging war against the law of my mind and making me a prisoner of the law of sin at work within my members. What a wretched man I am! Who will rescue me from this body of death? (Romans 7:21-24).

I sure can identify with Paul's anguish! You probably can too. But, my friend, there's hope! Paul gives us the answer to both his struggle and ours. You can almost hear him shout, "Thanks be to God—through Jesus Christ our Lord!...because through Christ Jesus the law of the Spirit of life set me free from the law of sin and death" (Romans 7:25; 8:2).

Jesus Christ has set us free to willfully and joyously serve Him and pursue His godly nature. So, as men who love the Lord and desire to influence others to do the same, let's point our spiritual compass toward home...toward God...toward eternity.

## The Value of Spiritual Discipline

Maybe you're reading along and thinking, *Why is this so important? Why go to all this trouble? What's the value?* Well, Paul must have known you would ask those questions, for he now tells us the value of spiritual discipline in a word—godliness: "Physical training is of some value, but godliness has value for all things, holding promise for both the present life and the life to come" (1 Timothy 4:8).

There's not a man reading this book who wouldn't agree that physical training has value—right? You know that physical exercise is beneficial for you. Paul would encourage you to go join a gym. Start walking. Lose a few pounds.

But don't stop with training just the physical realm, which has "some value." If you want what will *really* count, what will have a *lasting* impact, then put your main focus on your spiritual life. This will help you enjoy the best of both worlds. Spiritual discipline will help you in your present life—your marriage, your children, your job, your ministry, your testimony—and in your future life as well. Now that's value!

I hope you understand why spiritual discipline is such an important part of becoming a man who makes a difference. Spiritual maturity is a key element in the life of God's man. With that in mind, in the next chapter we will look at the steps you and I need to take to become more disciplined spiritually. But first, think through this challenge:

> You no more need a day off from spiritual concentration on matters in your life than your heart needs a day off from beating. As you cannot take a day off morally and remain moral, neither can you take a day off spiritually and remain spiritual. God wants you to be entirely His, and it requires paying close attention to keep yourself fit. It also takes a tremendous amount of time.[4]

*The world is full of naturally brilliant people
who never rise above mediocrity
because they will not make the sacrifice
which superiority requires.*[1]

*Without discipline we are not disciples,
even though we profess His name and
pass for a follower of the lowly Nazarene.
In an undisciplined age when liberty and licenses
have replaced law and loyalty,
there is greater need than ever before
that we be disciplined to be His disciples.*[2]

# Practicing Personal Discipline

*I beat my body and make it my slave so that…*
*I myself will not be disqualified for the prize.*

—1 CORINTHIANS 9:27

❧

There are many men who have influenced my life, but three men in particular have made a lasting impact.

First there was my father. My dad modeled a number of basic areas of discipline for me. He taught me the value of hard work, the need for thrift, and the reward of providing for your family. I owe a lot to my father's example and his many fatherly reminders about the importance of discipline.

Next was my scoutmaster. Mike was a successful executive at a local company. He had four girls, and I think he wished he had had a boy or two! So he went out into my neighborhood and recruited a group of little guys to form a scout pack and a basketball team. Mike taught us the discipline of working together as a team, whether we were pitching a tent in the woods or playing basketball. Every time I serve on a committee or tie a square knot, I think of Mike.

Then there was my pastor of more than 25 years, John MacArthur. I already shared a little of his influence on my life in an earlier chapter, but John drilled into me the value of disciplined Bible study, the importance of interpreting the Bible correctly, and a deep respect for the Word of God and its transforming power in a man's life.

Each of these men had a marked impact on my life. Each chiseled some facet of discipline into my character. Each man, too, in his own way and in his own sphere, is and was a man who made a difference. Each had or has had a lasting impact on others—my father on me, Mike on a rag-tag bunch of neighborhood boys, and John MacArthur on a church congregation and the world through his audio messages and books.

## The Journey Toward Discipline

It's been said that a journey of a thousand miles begins with a single step. Well, the journey toward spiritual discipline (and becoming a man who makes a difference) begins with a few first steps toward God. Let me share with you what those steps are.

Step 1: *Determine to become more disciplined*—If nothing I have said so far has motivated you to become more disciplined, then ponder the end result of strolling through life as an undisciplined person. Imagine the disappointment you will be to yourself, to God, and to your family if you fail to be the man you could have been simply because you didn't make the effort, because you took the easy road.

I'm sure you have heard the slogan "No pain, no gain." That slogan is usually posted in a gym or over a locker room door. But these same four words are also a perfect paraphrase of the personal philosophy of achievement of our man-of-influence, Paul. He said, "I beat my body and make it my slave so that…I myself will not be disqualified for the prize" (1 Corinthians 9:27). Discipline, whether in the spiritual or the physical realm, requires effort. But the effort is well worth it. You will receive a double prize—the eternal prize that Paul is talking about, and the earthly prize of accomplishment and impact.

Why not determine today that, with God's help, you want to emerge as a man of influence, as one who practices personal discipline as a lifestyle? Determine today that *you* will apply greater energy to the different roles that are required of *you*—your role as the spiritual head of your family, your role as a husband, father, provider, friend, and even son and son-in-law. Godly influence doesn't just happen without any effort. Discipline in any area of your life starts with desire. It takes time to develop the disciplines required for spiritual maturity and personal accomplishment, and it all starts with desire. And it starts today.

What is the level of your desire?

> What you are tomorrow,
> you are becoming today.

Step 2: *Develop spiritual sensitivity*—What does spiritual sensitivity mean? It means to walk through life with a God-consciousness. To be spiritually sensitive, you need to know how God would act, talk, and respond to life's situations. So how can you develop this kind of sensitivity?

One way is to read about God in the Bible. There, He has written about Himself. As you read the Bible, you begin to understand the nature and character of God. As you see how He responded graciously to His fallen creation and sacrificed His only Son for us, you begin to understand how you should be more loving, giving, and selfless. As you become more sensitive to spiritual truths, you become more discerning about the everyday issues you face in life.

Spiritual sensitivity means that you are always asking, "How would Jesus respond to this situation or this person?" Paul called this "having [the] attitude in yourselves which was also in Christ Jesus" (Philippians

2:5). So now the question becomes this: How can you develop this attitude or mind of Christ?

Years ago a great man of God named Harold Lindsell came to our church to conduct a seminar. Dr. Lindsell was a professor and author and had done much in his earlier days to defend the Christian faith against liberal thinking. It was quite evident throughout the one-day seminar that he really knew his Bible.

After the seminar I summoned up my courage, went to him, and asked how he came to know the Bible so well. I expected him to say it was his theological training or his ability to interpret Scripture. But, to my surprise, he said it was *a lifetime of regularly and systematically reading through the Bible that gave him his depth of understanding of God's Word.* That's pretty simple, isn't it? What a joy it was to realize that I, too, could have a solid grasp of God's Word! All it would take was the discipline of being faithful to read my Bible.

That seminar with Dr. Harold Lindsell lasted for only one day. But his influence produced a lifelong impact on me. Following his example, I have attempted to regularly read through God's Word for the past 25 years. (Does this story of my encounter with Dr. Lindsell help you better recognize the power of influence?)

Now, how are you doing in this area of your life? Are you disciplined? Are you consistent in your reading and studying of God's Word? Maybe you need to review Key #1 in chapters 3 and 4 to re-excite you about your Bible.

> Spiritual sensitivity means
> you can discern good from evil.

Step 3: *Improve your prayer life*—One evening while fulfilling my role as a deacon in my church, I met and interviewed a man and his wife for membership in our church. What a great couple! Well, one week later I was leading the prayer time for our Sunday school class and asked several different men to pray for the group's prayer requests. After the class was over, the man I had interviewed for membership came up to me. He was visibly shaken and pleaded with me to please never call on him to pray. He said he was not good at prayer.

Why is it so hard for some men to pray? Maybe the answer is as simple as this: We don't pray enough to feel comfortable praying with our wife and family or in a public meeting at church. But just like any of the other spiritual disciplines, the more you consistently do it, the more it will come naturally to you.

(And, by the way, this man and I started meeting and praying together. Today, most people in the church would consider him to be a man of prayer, both in private and in public. You and I, like my hesitant friend, can learn to pray simply by praying. If you've felt awkward about praying, find someone who will help you learn to pray. That's what the disciples did—they asked Jesus to help them!)

If prayer is still not a vital part of your life, maybe you need to review Key #2 in chapters 3 and 4.

---

"Lord, teach us to pray" (Luke 11:1).

---

Step 4: *Deal with your sin*—Remember our definition of *godliness* from the last chapter? Godliness is living like and for God. To do that we need to deal with our sin. *Sin* is a foreign word for most people today. Most will say, "I made a mistake," or "I committed an indiscretion." But to be a man of godly influence, you and I must recognize sin for what it is and confront it head on. Sin is anything that misses the mark, and that mark is the standard set by God Himself in His Word.

How can you live as a proper influence on others if you don't deal with sin in your life? You can't. But as the Bible states, "If we confess our sins, he is faithful and just and will forgive us our sins and purify us from all unrighteousness" (1 John 1:9). Confession of sin opens up the way for us to become the right kind of influence. And it's when we deal with our sin that we are developing our spiritual sensitivity, learning to discern what is right and what isn't.

How can we know when we've sinned? In the Bible, God tells us how He wants us to live. You can see again why it's so important that we read our Bible. You will never know when you are missing God's mark without knowing the instructions in "God's Rule Book." The Bible contains and communicates God's standards for your life. Dealing with sin is such an important part of being a man who makes a difference that we will study it in more depth when we get to Key #7 in chapters 16 and 17.

---

### Deal with your sin...or God will.

---

Step 5: *Worship with God's people*—Your first priority as a Christian man is to your physical family. God holds you accountable for being the spiritual leader of your family. That may seem scary, but the good news is that your leadership can begin with the easy, do-able step of taking your family to church. You set a godly example and have a tremendous influence on your family just by getting your family involved in church. So start with just attending church!

But your impact shouldn't stop with church attendance and your immediate family. You also have a responsibility to your spiritual family or your church family, the body of Christ. God calls you to take your family to church to *worship God,* and He also calls you to go to church to *serve God's people.* This service comes as we use our spiritual gifts. Spiritual gifts are God-given abilities that are entrusted to us at salvation so that we can minister to others in the church. First Corinthians 12:7 says each Christian's spiritual gifts are to be used "for the common good." We'll learn more in chapters 18 and 19 about our service to the people of God.

For now, simply make it a habit to cultivate the spiritual discipline of worshiping with God's people each week in a local church. Your example of weekly worship with God's people will have a profound impact on others—starting with your family! And don't forget to look for opportunities to serve others while you're there.

God created us to worship Him.

## Discipline and a Life of Impact

Over the last few chapters we've learned the great value of discipline, and I trust you are sensing the importance of discipline in a man's life. Whether it's Lance Armstrong, the apostle Paul, or the men who have impacted your life, the reason for their influence is their disciplined lifestyle. We could list and comment on many other spiritual disciplines that round out a man of discipline and influence—disciplines such as meditation, fasting, and giving tithes. But you've gotten a good start with the disciplines of reading your Bible, praying, dealing with sin, and attending church. Now we're going to move on and look at how discipline fleshes itself out in eight major areas of a man's life. But before we do, I'd like to share one final thought regarding discipline:

> While...failure may at times be due to limited ability, too often the deficiency is not in native endowment but in character. The capacity for grueling application is lacking. There may be the promising start, but not the discipline required to carry through. Even if by good fortune or "pull" the undisciplined man should reach the position of [influence], he cannot maintain it, for he is not inwardly prepared. He collapses under the weight of responsibility, and the pressure and complexity of detail. He lacks the strength of leadership, the fullness of knowledge, the soundness of judgment, which can only be built up bit by bit through years of painstaking toil.[3]

### *The Nature of Discipline*

- Discipline is a spiritual issue—*everything* done to the glory of God (1 Corinthians 10:31).

- Discipline has no shortcuts—no quick results.

- Discipline has no reserve—self-control must be reinstituted tomorrow.

- Discipline begins with the little things—like picking up your dirty socks.

- Discipline tackles the difficult thing—easy requires little.

- Discipline starts with the mind—"I will."

- Discipline proceeds with a mandate—"I must."

- Discipline never gets distracted—"This one thing I do."

- Discipline never takes a vacation—it's for life.

- Discipline is ever-changing—growth requires new disciplines to meet life's next and latest challenges.

## TEN KEYS TO A LIFE OF IMPACT

*Key #6*

# Goals

*The true value of your life and the extent of
your influence will be dependent on how
you develop your life, how you put the "raw
material" to use. Goals can help you to live out
the potential that God has placed in you.*
—JIM GEORGE

# Developing Lifelong Goals

*It has always been my ambition to preach the*
*gospel where Christ was not known.*

—ROMANS 15:20

❧

Aspiration is a good thing for us as men. Do you remember, as a young boy, dreaming about becoming a fireman, a policeman, a great athlete, an astronaut, a scientist, or a fighter pilot (that was my dream!)? These dreams may or may not have been realized at this point in your life. But dreams are not just for the young. And they are certainly not just for one phase of our lives! No, no matter what our age or station, we still need to have a passion, a deep desire, a focus, a direction for our lives. We need to ask ourselves constantly, "Where am I going with my life? Am I living out the right priorities? Are the things I'm doing today going to have a lasting impact on others?"

A key to answering these questions is understanding, as a Christian man, what it means to have godly ambition. You and I need to know what God is asking of each of us as a Christian man (and as a Christian husband if we are married, and as a Christian father if we have children, and so on). Normally God's calling for each of us is what's right in front of us. Where does God have you right now, today? That becomes your starting point for the rest of your life. Now you are ready to set the right goals—goals that will drive the rest of your life. These goals will help you to develop a life of influence for the glory of God.

## The Need for Godly Ambition

Ambition can be both positive and negative. I am sure you have been exposed to ambitious people who have scratched their way to the top and, in the process, left their claw marks on the backs of you and others whom they climbed over in order to reach their goal.

That's not the kind of ambition we want to talk about in this chapter. No, the kind of ambition we are talking about is a *godly* ambition. What do I mean by this? A godly ambition is a desire to serve God and to spend your life and energies fulfilling all His will (see God's comments about King David in Acts 13:22). A man of impact has goals and ambition, to be sure. But those goals and that ambition are not for himself. God's man strives solely for the glory of God and the good of others.

Paul is a perfect example of a man with godly ambition. From the day he received his commission from God to go to the Gentiles (Acts 22:21), he was relentless in his drive. Yet his drive had its focus in the will of God. Paul's focus is evident in his words, "I will come to you very soon, if the Lord is willing," and "I know that when I come to you, I will come in the full measure of the blessing of Christ" (1 Corinthians 4:19 and Romans 15:29).

Paul's ambition was to preach the gospel. He recruited and trained others who shared this goal as well, which enabled his influence to spread to many regions. When Paul wrote to his friends in Rome, he shared about his desire to go to places where others had not yet gone.

Why? Because he wanted to influence others with the gospel of Jesus Christ. He boldly penned, "It has always been my ambition to preach the gospel where Christ was not known" (Romans 15:20). In this case, the place Paul had in mind was Spain (Romans 15:24). The job of evangelism was getting done and God's will was being accomplished because Paul had lined up his ambition with God's calling for his life. In time, Paul desired to witness in Spain and to travel there by way of his friends in Rome.

Paul's example shows us that God's will, as mediated through our goals, can and should be a part of our life if we want to influence others. I believe this is part of what Paul had in mind when he said, "Follow my example, as I follow the example of Christ" (1 Corinthians 11:1). Let's follow Paul's example by bringing our ambition in line with God's will.

## Some Benefits of Having Goals

What are your goals in life? Have you defined them yet? You'll find that goals can help you in a lot of ways. For example...

- *Goals give definition*—Goals change your thoughts from daydreams and make them concrete. Goals are statements about the future—what you believe might be the will of God for you. Goals can then bring that future (if the *Lord* wills...or if it is the Lord's *will*!) into the present so you can do something about God's future in your life today.

- *Goals give focus*—Men tend to stay busy doing so many little things that they don't have time to focus on the big things and the important areas of life. But not Paul...or you! Paul stated in Philippians 3:13, "But *one* thing I do." Be sure your motto isn't "These *many* things I dabble in"!

- *Goals give motivation*—Goals are one of the most powerful motivational forces you can have in your life. They're what gets you out of bed at 5:00 a.m. They help excite and prod you along the way when you get weary. Read

what one gentleman said about the motivational power
of goals:

> Observing the lives of people who have mastered
> adversity, I have repeatedly noted that they have estab-
> lished goals and, irrespective of obstacles, sought with
> all their effort to achieve them. From the moment
> they've fixed an objective in their mind and decided
> to concentrate all their energies on a specific goal, they
> begin to surmount the most difficult odds.[1]

What a powerful force can be yours as you establish goals
based on what you believe to be the will of God, and
then allow the enabling power of the Holy Spirit to work
through you as you serve God and others!

- *Goals help in the decision-making process*—How do you
  make your decisions? Without goals, your decisions are
  likely to be influenced by the demands of others, or made
  by default (no other option), or on the spur of the moment
  (you just can't seem to think of a good reason to say no).
  But with goals—goals based on God's will for your life—
  you will have a much better idea of how to make the best
  decisions.

- *Goals help develop your life and impact*—I once read about
  a Ripley's "Believe It or Not" article that pictured a plain
  bar of iron worth $5. The story went on to say that if the
  same bar of iron were made into horseshoes, it would be
  worth $50. If it were made into needles, the value would
  be $5000. If it were made into balance springs for fine
  Swiss watches, it would be worth $50,000. The point of
  the story was that raw material gains value according to
  how that raw material is developed.

Friend, God has created you and me in His image. That
in itself settles our worth and our value! But we can still be

a little rough around the edges, still in the "raw material" stage. However, we have the potential to develop. We develop our life and put the raw material to use. And goals can help in the process. Won't you accept the challenge to develop your life and influence?

Dear man of God, goals are important and should be a constant, ever-evolving part of what God is doing in your life. As a Christian man, are you seeking God's direction and setting goals in your life—goals for your work, your family, and your personal growth? I'm sure you've heard the popular saying, "Aim at nothing and you will hit it every time." Don't drift through life without a course, a compass, or a cause. Others are depending on your leadership. So take aim...set your goals...hit the target! Make a difference and an impact! Make sure that when you die, people will know you were here.

## Eight Areas of Life That Call for Goals

Once you and I understand that life is but a "vapor" (James 4:14 NASB) and that soon we will be gone, determining our priorities becomes most urgent. Does that make you wonder what priorities you need to focus on? If so, I'm glad. Why? Because 97 percent of adults never write down their lifetime goals. Friend, I want you to be part of the 3 percent who do.

I believe you and I can streamline our priorities to eight major areas. We will start with two of the eight areas in this chapter, and finish the list over the next two chapters. And as we begin, I challenge you to prayerfully evaluate these eight areas of your life. Ask God to show you any weaknesses that need attention. And ask Him to show you the goals you need to set in these areas.

1. *Spiritual*—I'm sure you're thinking that I sound like a broken record. Well, maybe so. But your spiritual health is what determines whether you are a man who makes a difference. As we learned earlier, this is the starting point for a life of influence. You cannot impart to

others what you do not possess yourself. And the most important thing you can impart to others is your vibrant, growing life in Christ.

You and I must also realize that spiritual growth is not optional. We are commanded in Scripture to grow in grace and knowledge (2 Peter 3:18). If you have started working on this area of your life, you might want to step up your efforts. Spiritual exercise, like physical exercise, must be continuous if we want to remain healthy. You can never live on past spirituality. Here are some ways you can exercise yourself toward greater spiritual growth:

- Read your Bible daily.
- Pray daily for your family and friends.
- Lead your family in prayer and devotions.
- Go to church regularly.
- Find someone to disciple you.

Are you concerned that taking the time to focus on these spiritual disciplines will cause some other areas of your life to suffer? That won't happen. Why? Because when you take care of your spiritual life, all the other parts of your life fall neatly into place. The famous writer C.S. Lewis observed, "Aim at heaven and you will get earth thrown in."

2. *Mental*—It's been said that the mind is a terrible thing to waste. Your mind is like your muscles. Use your muscles and you increase in strength. Use your mind and you increase in your mental capabilities. I have heard statistics that say the average adult watches six hours of television a day. What a terrible waste! Watching that much television won't help us become men of influence. The Bible commands you to "be transformed by the renewing of your *mind*" so that you can know and do God's will (Romans 12:2).

How can you and I develop our mind? The best way is to *read*. I'm going to make a strong statement here and if you think about this carefully, I believe you'll find this to be true. *You will never be a leader in any area of your life if you are not a reader in those areas of life. You will never be a leader in your family, your job, your church, or your community if you are not a reader.* Brother, a reader is a leader…and a leader is a reader. It's as simple as that!

Why would I make such a strong statement? First, I have seen this principle proven in the lives of too many men to believe otherwise. And second, if you are not a reader and therefore keeping yourself informed, you will tend to be more dependent on others to help you in certain matters or situations.

Now, some dependency is not bad, because all of us can benefit from those who are knowledgeable in certain areas—such as a pastor, who can teach us the Bible, or a banker, who can give us important financial advice. But much of what others are eager to tell us is worldly and harmful, and can cause us to "conform" to the pattern of this world (Romans 12:2), as Paul said. But we're *not* to conform, but rather, to "be transformed by the renewing of your *mind*" (Romans 12:2). And the best way to renew your mind is to grow mentally as you feed upon the truths of God's Word.

When you are growing mentally, especially in the spiritual realm, your mind is being transformed. You are then "able to test and approve what God's will is" (Romans 12:2). You are steadily maturing and constantly training yourself to "distinguish good from evil" (Hebrews 5:14). This, in turn, will help you answer important questions such as, What is God's will for me and my family? What is good and what is evil?

Now, how can you become this mental man of impact? Start by picking up a book—the Book, the Bible—and start reading. Next, pick out a book that deals with one of the eight major areas of life and start reading. Start learning. Start growing spiritually and mentally. Start having an impact. Start creating a life of godly influence. And as time goes on, you can read other books that can help you grow stronger in the eight areas we are studying in this and the next two chapters.

*It concerns us to know the purposes we seek in life,
for then, like archers aiming at a definite mark,
we shall be more likely to attain what we want.*
—ARISTOTLE

# Defining Your Purpose

*One thing I do: Forgetting what is behind and straining
toward what is ahead, I press on toward the goal...*

—Philippians 3:13-14

August 31, 1974 was a red-letter day in my life. Wow! That was the day my wife and I sat down together and each wrote some lifetime goals. Up until that day, I had flopped and floundered and made little or no progress in achieving much of anything with a lasting godly influence. Basically I had spent the first 30 years of my life drifting from one desire to another...and most of the time, without God in mind.

But then, on that life-changing Sunday afternoon, I decided I needed to ask God to give Elizabeth and me wisdom as we sat down to write goals—goals that we hoped would line up with His will for our lives. Today, almost 40 years later, both Elizabeth and I are still operating our lives according to those goals that were written with hearts full of hope—goals that have simplified our focus in life, goals that have allowed me to influence not only my wife and children, but also fellow believers in my church and the Christian community nationally and internationally.

Why are goals such an important key to becoming a man who makes a difference? Because they help us to define our purpose. For you and me as "heaven-born souls," we "cannot without great peril be content to miss the smallest part of the Master's will"[1] and purpose for our lives. It's true that the poorest of all men is not the one without *gold*, but the one without a *goal*. As I learned from my own experience, life for a goalless man has no meaning and no purpose. There is little reason for living, and even littler impact! By contrast, goals give us direction, purpose, and help us know how to best use our time and energy—thus making us men of impact.

## Eight Areas of Life That Call for Goals

In the previous chapter we discussed two of the eight areas of life in which we ought to have goals—the *spiritual* and *mental* realms. Now let's press on and look at more areas in this chapter.

3. *Physical*—Vince Lombardi once said, "Fatigue makes cowards of us all." This legendary coach of the Green Bay Packers football team knew that "physical training is of some value" (1 Timothy 4:8). So did the apostle Paul. In fact, Paul wrote the words in 1 Timothy 4:8 regarding the value of physical training.

I'm sure you realize that people in America are known for being overindulgent in many ways…and that includes the physical realm. The average person in the United States is characterized as being overweight and in desperate need of exercise. However, as a man of influence, you must understand three truths:

—your body is a *stewardship* from God (1 Corinthians 6:19-20),

—your body is the *temple* of the Holy Spirit (1 Corinthians 3:16), and

—your body is meant to *glorify* God (1 Corinthians 6:19-20).

So how about a look in the mirror? How are you doing on your stewardship of God's temple, your body? Have you stepped on the scales today? When was the last time you did some physical exercise (other than walking to the refrigerator for another sandwich)? God cares about your body and health. Therefore you need to take care of yourself physically. Here are some suggestions (and notice that the first two deal with your spiritual life as well!):

- *Watch out for sin*—Psalm 32:3-5 tells us what happened to David's physical life when he failed to confess his sin. His body suffered, his bones wasted away, he suffered day and night, and his strength was sapped.

- *Walk by the Spirit*—One "fruit of the Spirit" you enjoy when you are walking in obedience to God's Word is "self-control" (Galatians 5:22-23). Self-control enables us to take better care of ourselves.

- *Weigh yourself every day*—If the arrow is pointing in the wrong direction, then go in the *right* direction by following the next suggestion.

- *Watch what you eat*—Paul said to "buffet" your body as in beat it—not "buffet" your body as in indulge yourself in a smorgasbord (1 Corinthians 9:27)! Watch both the quality and quantity of the food you take in (Daniel 1:12-15).

- *Work out regularly*—Get a little bit of physical training into your schedule—training that Paul said is of some value (1 Timothy 4:8).

- *Work at your stewardship*—You are not your own, and neither is your body. You were bought with a price—a high price!—by Jesus Christ. So be a good steward of it (1 Corinthians 6:19-20).

- *What you see is what you are*—Realize that your outward physical appearance reflects your inner spiritual condition. One picture is worth a thousand words! Do you like what you see?

- *Win the battle*—One of the apostle Paul's secrets to his life, his ministry, and his lasting impact is found in his battle cry regarding his body: "I...make it my slave" (1 Corinthians 9:27). Paul viewed his body as an opponent that had to be conquered at all costs...or else. Who's winning the battle for your body?

I have long followed the lives of leaders on every front, making the study of leadership a personal passion. In regard to the physical area, I particularly like what President Harry S. Truman, a no-nonsense politician from Missouri, observed: "In reading about the lives of great men, I found that the first victory they won was over themselves...self-discipline with all of them came first."[2] A man who makes a difference, a man of lasting impact, is marked as a man of rigorous personal physical discipline. May you (and I) be such a man!

4. *Social*—Before you get the wrong idea, let me clarify that by using the word *social* I'm not talking about your party life. No, I'm talking about your relationships. You and I are in constant contact with people—at home, at work, at church, in the community...and the list goes on. If we want to have an influence on others, we need to be careful that we are not guilty of having too many of the wrong friends and not enough of the right friends. We are to influence people rather than be influenced by the wrong people.

Now the question is, How do you determine the level of importance of these contacts? What's more, you also need to prioritize your contacts in the right order. To make sure you are on the right track, realize that there are four different types or levels of people whom you are to influence.

Level 1: Your family—Next to your relationship with Jesus Christ, family is your top priority. Never sacrifice your relationship with your family for any lesser relationships. Christ said, "What will it profit a man if he gains the whole world and forfeits his soul?" (Matthew 16:26 NASB). When it comes to my family, I apply Christ's words in a slightly different way: "What will it profit a man to gain the whole world and lose his *family*?" My family is precious to me, and I work hard daily at making sure, even now when my children are grown and gone, that they are Number One.

Level 2: Your friends—Friends are a gift from the Lord. You should cultivate friendships with other men, especially other Christian men—men who will encourage you in your faith and give good advice. The Bible says, "As iron sharpens iron, so one man sharpens another" (Proverbs 27:17). And friend, that's the kind of *friends* you need. What does such a friendship look like? For a good study of brotherly love and friendship, Jonathan and David give us a model to follow (see 1 Samuel 18 and 20). These two men of influence...

> assented to the same authority,
> knew the same God,
> were going the same way,
> longed for the same things,
> dreamed mutual dreams,
> yearned for the same experiences of holiness and worship.[3]

When it comes to you and your friendships, I think it goes without saying (but I will say it anyway), that *you should be extremely cautious in your associations with any woman other than your wife.* A married man shouldn't maintain the kind of friendship with a woman that he might normally maintain with other men. The danger is too great that such a friendship will end up becoming more than that. The Bible says when a man is attracted to a woman other than his wife, he's "playing with fire" (Proverbs 6:27-29). And brother, you are bound to get burned!

Level 3: Your workmates—You work alongside others every day, and if you want to be a man of influence, you'll want to make an effort to build relationships with your workmates. The closer they get to you, the more clearly they will see the image of Jesus Christ stamped on your life.

Remember, no contact equals no impact! (And again, be careful about the level of your interaction with women at work.)

Level 4: Your encounters with neighbors and strangers—Be friendly with everyone you encounter. Give a smile, a word of encouragement, a helping hand. Show them the love of Christ. Be a good neighbor. The same is true for neighbors as for workmates—no contact equals no impact.

When it comes to your social life, be willing to go to the ends of the earth, if needed, to find those relationships that will either pull you along or pull you up. And conversely, avoid at all costs (and like the proverbial plague!) anyone who would pull you down (1 Corinthians 15:33).

5. *Vocational*—In the book of Genesis we learn about the beginning of everything...including work. We read that "the Lord God took the man and put him in the Garden of Eden to *work* it and take care of it" (Genesis 2:15). Do you realize this scene took place before the fall of mankind to sin? That means that, contrary to popular belief, work is not a part of the curse. God did say after man's fall that our work would be more difficult, but God still wants you and me, as His men, to work and glorify Him (1 Corinthians 10:31). How can you, a man of impact, glorify God in your work?

- By providing for your family (1 Timothy 5:8).
- By seeing your job as a calling from God (Genesis 2:15).
- By striving for excellence (Colossians 3:23-24).
- By being content (1 Timothy 6:8).
- By submitting to your employer (Ephesians 6:5-8).

- By being a servant to others (Galatians 5:13).
- By being a good testimony with your life (2 Corinthians 3:2).

The quality of your influence is determined by the quality of your work. Therefore, my friend, do your work "with all your heart," as if you were "working for the Lord" (Colossians 3:23).

## Defining Your Purpose

Yes, August 31, 1974 was a red-letter day for me. It sent my life into warp speed...and in the right direction. And things have never slowed down. Not for one second! Why? Because, for the first time in my life, I had a purpose that went beyond me—way beyond me. The goals I wrote took me from being a *receiver* to being a *resource*. You see, in the past, my selfish desires were just that—selfish. But as I began to plan my life for the glory of God and according to His Word, I saw myself as one who could help others and be a resource for God in their lives.

Now, I must ask you: What is your purpose? Have you written some goals that would define your purpose? If not, it's never too late to start. Defining your purpose through goal-setting will give your life new purpose that God can use.

Before we move on to the next chapter and look at more areas of our lives for which we should develop goals, I want to encourage you with this list of benefits you can enjoy when you set goals.

- Goals help define the purpose of your life.
- Goals help develop a streamlined life.
- Goals help determine a focus for your life.
- Goals help drive each day of your life.
- Goals help display the stewardship of your life.
- Goals help design a life of influence.

*Where do you want to go in life?*
*How do you want to get there?*
*Do the roles you fill contribute to your goal?*
*What is really important that you do?*
*What merely fills up time?*
*In determining your best roles, keep those that*
*advance you toward your goal and*
*eliminate those that are useless and a drag.*
*Your trouble may be too many good roles.*
*You cannot afford to take on*
*more than you can handle well.*[1]

# Practicing God's Plan

*Do your best to present yourself to God as one approved,*
*a workman who does not need not be ashamed.*

—2 TIMOTHY 2:15

※

I t lasted only two hours, but when it was over, I had a golden set of goals for my life! I'm talking about that red-letter day I described in the last chapter. Well, writing the goals was the easy part. Next followed more than 30 years of practicing them! As I mentioned in the previous chapter, goals require a stewardship. Once I put on paper what I believed God was doing in my life as well as what He wanted me to do (and what I dreamed of doing for Him), I was then duty-bound to fulfill that stewardship. I, like Timothy in the scripture quote above, was being challenged to present myself to God as a good steward of the life He had given me.

My heart's desire is to be a workman who will not be ashamed when

I stand before my Lord someday—and I'm sure you feel the same way. And then I wonder, *How can I do my best to be that approved workman?* I think asking this question is a good first step for both of us. Once you and I have an answer, we can then take the next step and develop goals that will set us in the direction we need to go to become an approved workman. And finally, we can then follow through and practice God's plan.

All that will become possible when we know the areas of our lives in which we need to develop goals. So far we have covered the *spiritual, mental, physical, social,* and *vocational* areas of our lives. Now let's look at the last three areas: *financial, family,* and *ministry.* And remember, as important as it is to have an understanding of God's plan for your life through goals, it's equally important that you live out God's plan on a daily basis. That's a central secret to living a life of impact!

## Eight Areas of Life That Call for Goals

6. *Financial*—Do you remember I had said my father taught me about thrift? He also taught me how to manage the money I earned during my high school years. He and I made a deal with these terms: Whatever amount of money I saved from the weekly paychecks I earned, he would match. What a deal! Believe me, I got in the habit of working hard, going to the bank each week, and depositing a certain portion of my hard-earned money into my savings account. Then, at regular intervals, Dad would add his portion. It was my first-ever "matching funds" program. Dad trained me to save, and he trained me well.

But I haven't said anything yet about my wonderful Christian mother, who also had a great impact on my life. Whereas my dad taught me how to save, my mother taught me how to give. She would often quote Jesus' words, "Where your treasure is, there your heart will be also" (Matthew 6:21). The motto of her life was, "You can't outgive God!"

As you well know, we live in a very materialistic society. And if you and I are not careful, we can easily get caught up in the selfishness of materialism. The best way to blunt this curse of our culture is to practice the twin disciplines of saving and giving. Both disciplines benefit other people and not ourselves.

The practice of these two disciplines—saving and giving—has served me well over the years. By always having money set aside in a savings account, my family and I have been prepared for uncertain times. (Believe me, we've had to dip into the savings during many an uncertain time!) And by giving sacrificially to God's causes, I've been able to help others today and store up treasures that will last for eternity in heaven (Matthew 6:20).

Here now are five key suggestions for handling your finances. And notice the spiritual thread that intertwines even your financial life.

*Balance*—The writer of Proverbs 30:8-9 asked God to give him "neither poverty nor riches, but give me only my daily bread." Why? Because "otherwise, I may have too much and disown you and say, 'Who is the LORD?' Or I may become poor and steal, and so dishonor the name of my God." Not too little and not too much. Now *that's* having a balanced perspective on one's finances.

*Trust*—One of my biggest problems (and I'm sure you can identify) is trust. I wonder, *Can I trust God with my life and my finances?* Jesus answers, "Do not worry about your life, what you will eat or drink; or about your body, what you will wear" (Matthew 6:25). The writer of Proverbs adds this admonition: "Trust in the LORD with all your heart and lean not on your own understanding" (Proverbs 3:5). Friend, you can trust the Creator of all things with your finances!

*Maturity*—What if I said that your checkbook reveals where your heart is? That the way you handle your money is an indicator of your focus and spiritual maturity? Well, it's true! So take a look at your checkbook or credit card statement. What does it show? Large amounts of money spent on your pleasures, hobbies, and personal things? Or large amounts of money given to God for His work? It's been said that the difference between a boy and a man is the size and the price of his toys. Always remember that...

—How you use your money reveals where your heart is and who you serve (Matthew 6:21-24).

—"Where your treasure is, there your heart will be also" (verse 21).

—"No one can serve two masters" (verse 24).

—"You cannot serve both God and Money" (verse 24).

In fact, it's important for you to realize the money you have is not even your money! It's *God's* money, and you are simply a *steward* of His money. When you get to the point where you see yourself as a steward of God's money, then you will grow more mature in this difficult area of life.

*Contentment*—When it comes to our finances, we need to follow Paul's example. He was able to say, "I have learned the secret of being content in any and every situation" (Philippians 4:12). Try saying no to yourself in the "things" department. Try being content with what you have. Try being happy about what other people have. Try being content with "food and clothing" (1 Timothy 6:8). Try being content with "godliness" (verse 6). Now *that,* my friend, is "great gain," in both the financial department *and* the spiritual department (verse 8)!

*Budgeting*—When you make and keep a budget, you are exercising "self-control," a fruit of the Spirit (Galatians 5:22). A budget is a battle plan for curbing the lure of our needs-driven society. A budget helps you see more clearly how to properly manage God's resources. Ask any financial advisor what the first step to financial freedom is. I would be greatly surprised if you didn't hear, "Make a budget...and keep it!"

7. *Family*—Earlier I commented on the fact that your family is number one priority after your relationship with God. And if you are married, *it starts with your wife.* If you focus your love and attention on her, all other family relationships will fall into place. And your

relationship with your wife starts with your relationship with God, who is your Ultimate Priority. If you have a vibrant, growing relationship with God, you will have the Spirit's love to give in building a vibrant, growing relationship with your wife. Your love for God will overflow in love for your wife. When you love God, your love for your wife and family will come naturally as well—what a bargain!

How do we demonstrate God's love? You and I need to do something every day to show our love. It doesn't have to be much. Little things go a long way. If your relationship with your wife is anything like mine, any bit of initiative will be appreciated. Here are two sure-fire suggestions to get you started.

First, *plan a date night each week.* Get a babysitter and go to a local eatery and spend an hour or two talking over the week, planning the future, catching up on how you are each living out God's plan for your lives, and dreaming big dreams together. And if you really want to make a good impression…

Second, *volunteer to babysit the kids* while your wife goes shopping or takes a class at the church or a local college.

I can't tell you the number of men I know who have been highly successful in their jobs and have, in their retirement years, been remorseful that they neglected their wife and kids along the way up the corporate ladder. Commit yourself now to not sacrificing your relationship with your wife on the altar of corporate success. Then follow that up with a commitment to your children. If you are going to parent children, then you must shoulder the responsibility of being a godly, caring, seriously involved parent—a father who desires to be a godly influence.

And speaking of fatherly influence, Theodore Epp, the famed broadcaster from the Back to the Bible radio program, often said, "The one man who had the greatest effect on my life was my father. He taught me the necessity of absolute dependence on Christ for a useful Christian life." And then there is George Beverly Shea, the great soloist who sang at Billy Graham's crusades. He credits the spiritual counseling of his father as the greatest single influence on his life.

Fellow husband and father (and grandfather, if you have grand-children), you can retire rich and still be the poorest man on earth if you have lost your family in the process. So watch out! Keep your God-given priorities in focus—God...then your wife...then your children. And don't forget to honor your parents as well (Ephesians 6:2). It's never too late to begin living out God's plans for you. If you haven't been the kind of husband and father we've been talking about, then start today. Set goals toward becoming God's loving husband and God's caring and influential father. Then follow through and faithfully live out God's plan for you and your family.

8. *Ministry*—What does a godly man do? He serves! That's what the godly men of influence did in Acts 6:1-6. In the early church there was a need to provide food for the widows, so godly men—men "full of the Spirit and wisdom" (verse 3)—were appointed to take care of the physical needs of these widows.

You and I are to serve others as well. As believers in Christ, we have been spiritually re-created by God to serve Him and His people. The Bible calls our service "good works" (Ephesians 2:10), and we are expected to serve other members of the church, the body of Christ (Galatians 6:10). The good news is that service and good works is a ministry you can have today, right now. You need no training to be a servant. So *serve!*

But beyond the good works of physical service, we as men of God are also called to discover and use, for the good of the church, what the Bible calls "spiritual gifts" (1 Corinthians 12:1-7). These "gifts" are spiritual enablements given to Christians through the ministry of the Holy Spirit (verse 7).

How can you know what your spiritual gifts are?

- *Ask God about your spiritual gifts*—Ask Him for wisdom as you seek to serve.

- *Ask to serve*—Begin by serving. Serve anyone and everyone. Be faithful and grow spiritually. As you serve in ministry, you will discover your areas of giftedness. Like

physical talents and abilities, spiritual gifts are discerned
and developed as they are being used.

- *Ask others about your spiritual gifts*—What are others seeing as the fruit of your ministry? Don't be afraid to ask
  others what they observe.

- *Ask yourself about your spiritual gifts*—In what areas of
  ministry do you enjoy serving most? Which avenue of
  service brings the greatest blessing to others?

As I review what I've written about the eight areas of our life that
ought to have goals, I can't help but think of a teaching from the ancient
Greeks. They were concerned with the development of the whole man.
They saw a man as less than whole if any part of the body, soul, or spirit
was undeveloped. I think we can safely say that setting goals and practicing God's plan for these eight areas will make you not only a whole
man, but a man of influence and lasting impact.

## Setting Goals for Your Life

Well, friend (and here I am, saying it again!), sitting down on that
Sunday afternoon and developing a life of focus with a handful of goals
was truly a turning point for me. I shudder to think what the past 30-
plus years might have been like without those goals. If you don't already
manage your daily life with the help of some lifetime goals, I pray that
you will do what I did. As a former pharmacist, here's another prescription for you:

℞   Pray and seek God's guidance.

℞   Set your goals.

℞   Review them often.

℞   Focus on them daily.

I guarantee that setting goals for your life and practicing them will
benefit you and everyone you know. Your influence will be greatly
enhanced if you do. This has been true for me, and I've seen it in the

lives of others. Setting and following such goals will, by God's grace, add up to a life of impact.

Now, I ask you…

> *What kind of leadership influence can you have on others if you don't first know where you are going? The man who makes a difference knows where he is going and how to get there. And others will gladly follow him there.*

That's why Key #6, Developing Lifelong Goals, is so important. It goes hand in hand with Key #4, Mastering Life's Challenges. Are you ready for the challenge? Your family, friends, church, and fellow workers are waiting for your leadership. In what direction will you lead?

*Key #7*

# Purity

*You live in a world awash with sensual images*
*available twenty-four hours a day....*
*But God offers you freedom from the slavery of sin*
*through the cross of Christ, and*
*He created your eyes and mind with an ability*
*to be trained and controlled.*
*We simply have to stand up and*
*walk by His power in the right path.* [1]

# Dealing with Temptation

*No temptation has seized you
except what is common to man.
And God is faithful; he will not let you be tempted
beyond what you can bear.
But when you are tempted,
he will also provide a way out so that
you can stand up under it.*

—1 Corinthians 10:13

Meet Augustine, a man who lived during the decline of the Roman Empire (AD 354–430). He was the Bishop of Hippo in northern Africa. Augustine contributed much to our understanding of the theology of the New Testament and is considered one of the greatest and most influential leaders in all of church history.

Now, Augustine was not always a man of godly influence. Like Paul, Augustine had a past. But unlike Paul, Augustine's past was sordid and littered with sensuality, immorality, and religious skepticism. His life of dissipation and pleasure was taking him nowhere, and his impact on others was purely negative.

Like the apostle Paul, Augustine had a dramatic conversion. And like Paul, Augustine experienced a complete turnaround in his life's direction. Paul turned from the life of a prideful religious Pharisee to a life of humility and faithful service for the cause of Jesus Christ. Augustine turned from being a womanizer and a pleasure-seeker to a life of ministry, becoming one of the great defenders of the orthodox Christian faith.

Augustine's personal experience with sin and God's great grace lent intensity and realism to his writings—so much so that readers more than 1000 years later (such as Martin Luther, the driving force of the Protestant Reformation) were deeply impacted. Augustine's turnaround and subsequent victorious Christian life illustrates yet another key quality in the life of a man who makes a difference—he deals with temptation.

## Two Men, Two Choices, Two Paths

There are a myriad of thoughts penned on the importance of choices. You've probably heard this one—

> Little choices determine habit;
> Habit carves and molds character
> Which makes the big decisions.

Or how about this one? "Choice, not chance, determines human destiny."

To see these truths lived out, meet two men...who made two choices...that led to two paths and two destinies.

*Cain*—Man #1 was Cain, the firstborn son of Adam and Eve. Cain and his brother Abel brought gifts to God, and their gifts received two different responses from God. Abel and his gift were pleasing to God, but Cain and his gift were not (Genesis 4:1-8).

What happened when God judged against Cain's gift? Cain had two choices for his response—he could either come before God and humbly ask forgiveness for himself and the nature of his gift, or he could become angry with God because of the rejection. Unfortunately, Cain chose the latter, less noble response. God then warned Cain about his wrong attitude and its potential consequences, saying, "Sin is crouching at your door; it desires to have you, but you must master it" (verse 7).

Two men, two choices, two paths. What choice did man #1 make? Cain chose to allow sin to master him and failed the test for handling temptation God's way. His jealousy toward his brother Abel and God's acceptance of Abel's gift caused Cain to sink deeper into sin and ultimately to murder his brother. In the end, Cain's choice to fall into temptation disqualified him from God's blessing and from any influence for good with his life. His choice led him down a path of destruction.

*Jesus*—Man #2 lived thousands of years after the days of Cain and Abel. This man, too, faced temptation. This man was Jesus. After 40 days of fasting, when Jesus was in a physically weakened state, He was tempted by Satan in three different areas of life. In all three temptations, Jesus fought back, quoting the Word of God (Luke 4:1-12). Jesus chose to withstand the temptations. He passed the tests perfectly and thus walked the path of positive influence, impacting the entire world—the path that led to the cross, the path that led to your salvation and mine. The tale of these two men looks like this:

| Two Men: | Cain | Jesus |
|---|---|---|
| Two choices: | gave in | withstood |
| Two paths: | murdered brother | saved many |
| Two results: | destruction | impact |

## Your Choice, Your Path

The choices of these two men give you and me some sobering lessons on the importance of dealing with temptation and sin. Did you notice that I wrote both *temptation* and *sin*? That's because they're different. Temptation is *not* sin. Cain was tempted—sin was "crouching at the door." He *could* have chosen to resist the temptation and therefore not to sin, but *didn't*. Jesus was tempted, but He *did* resist the temptations.

How about you? How are you dealing with your past, your thoughts, your temptations? Where are your choices leading you? What direction is your path taking you? I'm sure that you, like me, are not always pleased with the way you handle (or fail to handle!) temptation.

Take heart, my fellow struggler. God has provided a way for us to stand up under the struggle against temptation and choose the path of influence. As 1 Corinthians 10:13 says, "God is faithful; he will not let you be tempted beyond what you can bear. But when you are tempted, he will also provide a way out so that you can stand up under it."

## God's Provision for Our Temptations

*First, God has provided a new law*—A law is a fixed way in which things work. For instance, the law of gravity says that anything heavier than air will fall. That means that if you jump off a ten-story building, you will fall to your death. But there are laws that counter the law of gravity—for example, the laws of aerodynamics. These laws allow a 747 jumbo jet, filled with hundreds of people and weighing hundreds of thousands of pounds, to fly.

In like manner, when you and I come to Christ, God counters the law of sin and death—a law that gave us no choice but death. Yet when we come to a saving knowledge of Jesus Christ, we come under the influence of a new law—the law of the Spirit of life in Christ (Romans 8:2). This new law sets us free from the bondage of sin. Through this new law, we now have the power to choose to resist temptation.

*Second, God has provided a guide*—A guide is someone or something that leads you through unfamiliar territory and keeps you from getting lost. Jesus promised He would give believers a guide to live in them and always be with them. That guide is the Holy Spirit, who lives in all believers and leads them into all truth (John 16:13). When you and I came to Christ, this promise from Jesus became true for us. As a result, we now have our own guide—the Holy Spirit—who leads us throughout all of life and all the situations we face.

*Third, God has provided a guidebook*—God has also given us our own personal guidebook, the Bible. Everything we need to know about life and godly living is presented to us in God's Word (2 Peter 1:3). This guidebook gives us the answers for dealing correctly with every kind of temptation.

*Fourth, God has provided guides*—God has also provided us with other believers who can encourage us to resist and overcome the temptations of this world. That's why it is so important for you to attend a local church. There you can find other more mature men who can hold you accountable and guide you with wise counsel. I am personally thankful to God for the many men of influence who have served as faithful, caring guides to me. These "soldiers of the cross" have been and are committed to watching over my spiritual growth on the battlefield of life.

Now, you may be thinking, *But Jim doesn't know my situation. He can't know the pressures I'm under—pressures on my job, in my marriage, with my children, from the baggage of my past life of sin. I can't help but succumb to temptation. No matter how hard I try, I can't seem to overcome certain sins!*

Well, you're right. I don't know what specific issues you are struggling with. But I do know that you are not alone. Temptation is universal. The Bible says it is "*common* to man" (1 Corinthians 10:13). That means you and I and all other men struggle with the same temptations and sins. That's the bad news.

But the good news is that God has provided a way out, an escape and victory (1 Corinthians 10:13 and 15:57). With these four resources—

> a new law (life in Christ),
>
> a guide (the Holy Spirit),
>
> a guidebook (the Bible),
>
> and guides (wise counselors)—

we have the ability to withstand the temptations that confront us in our daily living. Statements of "I can't" no longer apply to us. Now, in Jesus Christ, it's "I can!" Paul tells us to "be strong in the Lord, and in his mighty power" (Ephesians 6:10).

So the next time you are confronted with an opportunity to sin (like in the next millisecond!), remember, "I *can* do everything through him who gives me strength" (Philippians 4:13). God has given you the *I can* to deal with that temptation. But you must supply the *I will*. It's your choice. Your path and your impact is at stake!

No choice is a small choice.

And no choice is a meaningless choice.

## The Devil Made Me Do It

Before we move on to the next chapter to learn about the practical aspect of fighting the battle of temptation, there's one more issue we need to address—the matter of shifting the blame.

Have you ever heard the statement, "The devil made me do it"? For most of us the devil is a convenient "fall guy." We blame him for our bad conduct, our wrong actions, and our failures. Everything is the devil's fault, not ours. Therefore you and I don't have to be responsible. Why should we, if we think the devil is responsible for our wrong behavior? It's like the lady who told the famous preacher, Donald Grey Barnhouse, after he informed his congregation they could no longer blame Satan for all their problems: "Dr. Barnhouse, I was disappointed in the message. You said we can't blame Satan. But Satan has always been such a comfort to me."

No, the devil doesn't make us sin. He doesn't need to! Oh, he may assist us by providing the gasoline, but we supply the wood! He's a great one to facilitate our sin. In most cases he merely provides the opportunities with his worldly schemes. And we, who so often find it hard to say no to sin and our flesh, willingly do the rest.

Suffice it to say, you and I should never again say, "The devil made me do it." It just isn't true!

So what can we do? How can we handle temptation? Don't fail to read the next chapter and its lifesaving message about how to handle three different types of temptation.

*Fortune. Fame. Power. Pleasure.*
*When it comes to temptation, these are the biggies.*
*These…represent the weakest links in our chain of*
*resistance…the most obvious chinks in our armor.*
*If the enemy of our souls wants to launch*
*one of his "flaming missiles"*
*toward an area that will have the greatest impact,*
*he's got a choice of…targets.*[1]
—CHARLES SWINDOLL

# Fighting the Battle Against Temptation

*Put on the full armor of God so that
you can take your stand...*
—Ephesians 6:11

∾

"War is hell!"

That's the quote I often heard from my dad, who was a soldier who fought in Germany during World War II. But a generation later, as I sat in a classroom at Fort Bragg, North Carolina, I was hearing it again...and beginning to feel the full force of the words, "War is hell!"

How did I come to be sitting in a classroom at Fort Bragg listening to a lecture on warfare? My U.S. Army Reserve medical unit was called up for active duty during the Bosnian crisis in the 1990s. We were on our way to Germany to take over the duties of a regular Army hospital corps that had been deployed to the battlefront in Bosnia. So there I sat, receiving a combat briefing. I was listening to instructors lecture on land mines, snipers, mortar attacks, chemical warfare, and so on. It was clear that the Army wanted to prepare our group for any and every danger we might face in battle.

## Life Is a Battle

Living the Christian life is a battle, too. (And if you don't think so, then you just might not be living the Christian life very successfully!) Jesus Himself told us, "In this world you will have trouble" (John 16:33). That trouble for us men comes in a variety of packages. And, like my Army instructors, God wants to prepare us for the inevitable battle. For us to be properly prepared, we must know what God's Word, the Bible, says about the temptations we will face as we go through life.

Most of us don't need a reminder of the temptations we struggle with every day. But, just in case you or I have forgotten what they are, the Bible gives us a list. Galatians 5:19 says, "The acts of the sinful nature are obvious"—and then the list reads:

> sexual immorality, impurity and debauchery; idolatry and witchcraft; hatred, discord, jealousy, fits of rage, selfish ambition, dissensions, factions and envy; drunkenness, orgies, and the like (Galatians 5:19-21).

Pretty awful, isn't it? So how can we get a handle on these temptations and fight the battle against them? Knowing how to deal with temptation and gaining the victory will go a long way toward ensuring that we will become men who make a difference! I am most grateful to Dr. Curtis Mitchell, now retired from Biola University, La Mirada, California, for grouping temptations into three types.

### Type A: Temptations of the Flesh

We as men are bombarded with *all* of the temptations in God's list in Galatians 5:19-21 *all* of the time. But I'm sure you agree that sensual and sexual temptation—Type A temptation—is a frequent and critical problem for Christian men today and a universal problem for every man. You and I can hardly take a step or live a minute without being assaulted with a Type A temptation, which is mainly triggered through the "eye gate." That makes the children's song lyric—"be careful, little eyes, what you see"—especially applicable for this type of sin…a line that would have helped the Old Testament king, David!

David, who sinned with Bathsheba, is a perfect example of a man who struggled with a Type A temptation (see 2 Samuel 11:1-5). What happened? The Bible explains it this way: David "*saw* a woman bathing. The woman was very beautiful [how did he know this, other than by a lingering look?] and David *sent* someone to find out about her" (verses 2-3)…and, well, you know the rest of the story. "David sent messengers to *get* her…and he *slept* with her" (verse 4).

Here's what I want you to notice: David's sin started with the eyes (which is true for many of the Type A temptations). David could have stopped the process at any time, but he *chose* (there's that word again) to proceed and to sin sexually with Bathsheba. He made the wrong choice. In fact, he made a *string* of wrong choices!

Now, how can you and I protect ourselves against Type A temptations, and especially those of a sensual nature?

First and foremost, always remember that God has provided "a way of escape" (1 Corinthians 10:13 NASB). Then follow these practical suggestions for defending yourself.

- *Pursue godliness*—The best defense is a good offense. Therefore pursue a life of godliness (2 Timothy 2:22). How? By reading God's Word, worshiping with God's people, and being accountable to one or more of God's men. Don't be a defenseless, defeated warrior. Don't give in to the temptation. Fight the battle for your purity with all the resources God has provided.

- *Avoid places and situations where you might experience temptation*—Stay away from old haunts and magazine racks with sensual covers on display. Don't be alone with a woman other than your wife (does that sound familiar?). "*Flee* the evil desires of youth" was Paul's advice to his young disciple (2 Timothy 2:22). And brother, it's good advice for you and me as well!

- *Avoid people who might tempt you*—I spoke earlier of "friends" who pull you down. Be careful about buddies from the past and friends from the present who have a lower standard than you do. Avoid anyone who might drag you down. Follow this wise advice from the book of Proverbs (known as "the book of wisdom") and keep your path far from them. "If sinners entice you, do not give in to them...do not go along with them, do not set foot on their paths" (Proverbs 1:10,15).

- *Avoid allowing your eyes to roam*—I used to have a sales manager who, as I would describe it, could undress a woman with his eyes. Don't be that kind of man. Determine to do what Job did when he "made a covenant with [his] eyes not to look lustfully at a girl" ( Job 31:1).

Type A temptations arise from the desires of our flesh. You and I don't need a lot of help from the devil with this type of temptation! No, our own sinful flesh spurs us along.

### Type B: Temptations of the World

Whereas Type A temptations are usually sensual and of the *flesh*, Type B temptations go deeper into the *heart*. Whereas Type A temptations usually involve *girls*, Type B temptations usually involve *gold* and *glory*—the temptations that relate to life and living. This type of appeal is called "the boasting of what [a man] has and does" and "the boastful pride of life" (1 John 2:16 NASB).

So often you and I are tempted with desires for money, possessions, and pleasures. These Type B temptations rob us of a heart and a passion for God and the things of God. Here's how they work...

In terms of generational categories, I am what's frequently described as a baby boomer. My parents came out of World War II with nothing but dreams of a better life for themselves and for me. I grew up with a focus on "the good life." That obsession, if you please, led me away from the Lord. Years later I recognized the emptiness of such a lifestyle. Then, like the prodigal son in the Bible, I realized how far away I was from God and returned home to a forgiving heavenly Father (Luke 15:11-32).

What a trap our materialistic society can lay for us! Now, don't get me wrong. Perhaps you have successfully handled these kinds of worldly temptations. But I didn't. And we can all fall, so…just be careful!

Now meet Lot. His story gives you and me an archetype of a Type B temptation. You'll want to read Genesis 13:1-13 for the whole story. But in a nutshell, Lot, who was Abraham's nephew, was given a choice of where to live and raise his herds. The Bible says Lot "looked up and *saw* that the whole plain of the Jordan was well watered…So Lot *chose* for himself the whole plain of the Jordan" (verses 10-11).

Do you want to hear God's comment on Lot's choice? He records, "Now the men of Sodom were *wicked* and were *sinning* greatly against the LORD" (verse 13). (Have you ever heard of Sodom and Gomorrah?!) While Lot's choice may have seemed to be the right business decision from a *practical* standpoint, it led to *spiritual* disaster for him and his family (see Genesis 19).

So what's to keep you from falling into the same trap that Lot (and I) fell into—Type B temptations—temptations of worldliness and materialism?

- *Develop a love for God* that withstands the pull of the world. Love grows with familiarity, so become familiar with God through reading His Word. "The love of wealth makes bitter men; the love of God, better men."[2]

- *Understand the lie* that the pleasures of this world are worth giving up what really matters…like your relationship with God, your family, your reputation, and your influence. Understand that the world is ebbing away, but doing the will of God has eternal rewards (1 John 2:17).

- *Realize the spiritual implications* that every decision, including business decisions, can have. Remember Lot!

- *Guard against* an unhealthy focus on "the good life." Theologically, wealth has the potential to create more serious problems than poverty does.

- *Remember* that you cannot serve the world and God at the same time (Matthew 6:24). A man of influence seeks the kingdom of God first (verse 33).

- *Realize* that the more encumbered you are with the world, the less freedom you have to serve God. As missionary Albert Sweitzer discovered, "Anything you own that you cannot give away, you don't own it, it owns you."

- *Pray daily* that God would give you the wisdom and strength you need to fight against worldliness. "It is the daily drill which makes the battle hero."[3]

### *Type C: Temptations of the Devil*

Do you remember my comment earlier that the devil is blamed for a lot of our temptations? As well as my statement that we are quite capable of sinning on our own, especially when it comes to Type A and Type B temptations? Well, Type C temptations are more directly involved with the devil. These are the temptations of the *soul.* These are temptations that frequently deal with the nature and character of God, that think ignoble thoughts about God. Let me illustrate...

Eve, the mother of all, was created and placed in the Garden of Eden to serve as Adam's helper and life partner (Genesis 2:18-22). Then some time later, when Eve was alone, she was approached by the serpent, who proceeded to tempt her to doubt God's character. Satan queried, "Did God *really* say...?" (Genesis 3:1). Satan planted seeds of doubt in Eve's mind regarding God's character and His instructions until she gave in, disobeyed God, and ate of the forbidden fruit.

Ever since that day, Satan has continued to ply his schemes to get us to mistrust God. So how do we deal with these kinds of temptations?

- *Gain a better understanding of God's attributes and His character*—We learn what God is like by reading His Word. When we don't read His Word, we tend to forget what He is like and fail to trust Him. And Satan loves a man with "spiritual amnesia"!

- *Gain a better understanding of Satan's tactics*—Satan loves to confuse people when it comes to theology (the study of God). If he can get you and me to have a distorted view of God, then chances are he can get us to have a distorted view of life, our conduct, and our accountability to a holy God. Instead, you and I must "be strong in the Lord and in his mighty power. Put on the full armor of God so that you can take your stand against the devil's schemes" (Ephesians 6:12).

- *Gain a better understanding of God's Word*—Build an arsenal of Scripture verses to use whenever you are tempted. Jesus fought the devil with the Word of God, constantly saying, "It is written…It is written…It is written" (Matthew 4:4-7). Are you well armed? Do you know *what* is written? Are you fighting your battles against temptation with the sword of the Spirit, which is the Word of God (Ephesians 6:17)?

## Seeking God's Help in the Battle

Brother, let's agree to fight the battle against temptation with our eyes wide open! Here are the cold, hard facts: Temptation is ongoing. As long as you and I are alive and breathing, we will encounter sin and temptation on every level—Type A, Type B, and Type C. The battle is raging in every area of your life and will ultimately be fought at every stage of your life. Whether you are a young man struggling with the temptations of the flesh, a middle-aged man tempted by worldliness and desires for fame, fortune, and "the good life," or a man in his sunset years who begins to doubt the sufficiency of God's promises and provision as you contemplate death, you (and every man) can be certain the temptations will never go away.

The question is this: Will you allow God to fight your battle for you through the resources He has given you? Or will you try to go it alone? Your future is riding on how you deal with temptation. *How you and I handle our temptations will drastically affect our ability to impact others for God.*

*Key #8*

# Service

*Tied to the value of the person
is the principle of servanthood.
We value what we freely serve.*[1]
—Douglas Groothuis

# Nurturing the Heart of a Servant

*Surely you remember, brothers,*
*our toil and hardship; we worked night and day*
*in order not to be a burden to anyone*
*while we preached the gospel of God to you.*

—1 Thessalonians 2:9

O ne nice feature of Southern California is the weather. Normally the climate is mild, even during the winter months. But on one particular day in mid-January, the weather was unusually cold and rainy. But more than the abnormal weather conditions, what made this an especially memorable day was the sad scene I witnessed at a cemetery. I was there because, several days earlier, a local funeral home called and asked me to officiate at a graveside service for a man who didn't have a pastor or a church in the area. I was eager to participate because I saw this as an opportunity to help out the man's family and to share the good news of Jesus Christ with those who attended.

When the day arrived, I made sure I got to the cemetery early so I could meet the man's family and friends and give them some words of encouragement in the midst of his death. The funeral director met me and the two of us began our graveside vigil. Finally, well past the time for the service to begin, a lone car came through the gate of the cemetery and stopped on the road that led to the casket, which rested under a canopy. In the car was the wife of the deceased.

Hurrying out of the car, the out-of-breath woman asked how long the service would last. She announced that she didn't have much time, and besides, she explained, her late husband hadn't had much time for anyone either. And now, as was obvious, no one had time for him or his service. I conducted the service in the driving rain with only the funeral director and the impatient wife present.

## What a Difference a Life Makes!

Now contrast the above scene with another funeral I participated in. Stan Miller had served as a pastor and hospital chaplain for more than 40 years. Stan was a man with a heart for serving. At his memorial service dozens of people—including his wife, children, grandchildren, and great-grandchildren—stood up and gave testimony to the impact Stan had on their lives. He had sacrificially loved his wife for more than 50 years. He had sacrificed for the education of his children. And he had continually sacrificed his time, money, and energies for others. The room was filled with hundreds of others, including myself, who had been impacted by Stan's life of service.

Like I said, this was quite a contrast to the other funeral!

—The first man was a taker his whole life and left nothing behind. As I drove away from his grave site, I looked into my rearview mirror and, from all appearances, there was little visible proof that the man had ever existed.

—The other man was a giver his whole life and left a legacy of influence behind. Hundreds were living proof of the lasting impact of his life of service.

That's the next key to the man who makes a difference—a man who makes an impact has a heart for serving others.

## Two Examples of a Servant

Serving others is not that easy. Our sinful flesh doesn't want to serve. Rather, it wants to be served! Servanthood is not seen as the "manly" thing to do. The world sees a servant heart as a weakness. But in Christianity a servant heart is highly regarded.

During the time my wife and I have been members of our present church, we have witnessed this heart for service in the lives of the church leaders. And I also have to say that over the years, I have been fortunate to see this mark of influence demonstrated by numerous other men in roles of leadership. Now let's look at two incidents involving two men of influence who give us what I believe to be the best demonstrations of what it means to have a heart for serving. And I think you will agree these were not weak men, but men of strength and men who obviously had a great impact.

*Jesus Christ*—I'm sure you agree that Jesus Christ was the most influential man who ever lived. No one has ever or will ever have the impact on history that this one man has had. Why? There's one very important reason—Jesus Christ was deity in human flesh. But as you read your New Testament, you don't see God-the-Son as an autocrat, a leader running roughshod over people or demanding respect and obedience. No, you see just the opposite! You see a humble servant.

Now, try to place yourself in this scene. In John chapter 13, we see God, in human flesh, taking a towel and a basin of water and kneeling down before His creation, His followers, and His subordinates, and washing their dirty feet. This has to be one of the greatest examples of servanthood ever recorded in history!

Sometime when you're having your devotions, read John 13:1-17 to get the full effect of this example of a servant's heart in action. Jesus' message to His disciples—and to us!—is this: "I have set you an example that you should do as I have done for you" (John 13:15). How could we not obey? So I ask you, Whose feet could you wash today? Who in your family needs you to come alongside as a servant? Who at church craves the helping hand of your service?

*Dwight L. Moody*—A second man who demonstrated the heart of a servant is the famous nineteenth-century Chicago preacher, D.L. Moody.

One year in the late 1800s, a large group of European pastors came to Moody's Northfield Bible Conference. The European pastors, following their custom of the time, put their shoes outside their rooms the first night to be polished by the "hall servant." But, the conference being in America, there were no hall servants.

That night, as Moody walked the halls of the dormitory praying for the conference and those in attendance, he saw the shoes. Not wanting to embarrass his visitors, Moody mentioned the need to some young ministerial students...who piously excused themselves from helping. So the world's most famous evangelist of his day returned to the dorm, gathered up the dirty shoes, took them to his room, and cleaned and polished them himself. The deed would have gone unnoticed except for the entrance of a friend who witnessed the event.

The next morning, the European pastors opened their doors to find shiny, spotless shoes. Moody told no one what he had done. But his friend told a few people, and then an amazing thing happened. During the remainder of the conference, different men secretly volunteered each night to shine the shoes of their guests.

Both Jesus Christ and D.L. Moody are prime examples of men who had a heart for serving. Both were men of true greatness and influence. Both demonstrate for us the impact a man can have when he develops a heart for serving others.

## Insights on Becoming a Servant

I hope you're catching the spirit of what it means to be a man who makes a difference. And I hope you now see how being a servant is key to having an impact. As I said at the outset of our profiling journey, the apostle Paul is always an excellent person to examine and re-examine as a man of profound influence. The impact of his life is still being felt today. Why? Because he, like his Master, Jesus, and like the great D.L. Moody, was a man with a heart for serving others.

So consider these insights on becoming a servant from the heart and life of Paul. Let's join up with him in Acts 17:2. Here, we learn that Paul spent "three Sabbath days" reasoning from the Scriptures with the Jews in the local synagogue in Thessalonica, a town in Macedonia (now Greece). We don't know exactly how much longer Paul was there because (as usual!) the Jews became jealous, started a riot, and forced Paul to leave town. Listen now as Paul reflects on his time with the Thessalonians. And pay close attention as he gives us nine insights on being a servant, as stated in 1 Thessalonians 2:1-12.

Insight #1: *Serve for a higher purpose*—Sometimes we do an act of service and then get the feeling that our service didn't count…that nobody noticed or cared…that it really didn't matter…that the whole thing was a failure. But that's okay! Paul had all the same feelings, yet he wrote, "You know, brothers, that our visit to you was not a failure" (1 Thessalonians 2:1). In other words, service for a higher purpose— for God's purposes—is never a failure, no matter what!

Do you remember the man Mordecai in the Old Testament book of Esther? Mordecai was the cousin of Queen Esther. And one day, while Mordecai was sitting in the gate (a place of influence in those days), he overheard word about a plot to kill the king. He then informed Esther… who informed her husband, the king, giving the credit to Mordecai… and the plot was foiled. How much time passed before Mordecai was recognized for his service to the king? Five long years later, the king realized that Mordecai had not been properly rewarded! Could you wait five years to be thanked for your service? Would you continue to serve even if it seemed your service went unnoticed or appeared to be a failure?

Here's Paul's message to us: If you and I serve for a higher purpose, God's purpose, then results or thank yous or recognition and rewards don't matter. Why? Because our service was done unto God. And that's our higher purpose—to please God. That's all that matters. John Whiteley, a nineteenth-century missionary to New Zealand, got it right when he penned these words:

> I thank God that I can say my duty is my delight, and the encouraging proofs I have that I do not labor in vain or spend my strength for nought encourages me to "Labour on at God's command, and offer all my work to Him."[2]

Insight #2: *Serve in spite of your situation*—In other words, if you or I wait until conditions are perfect, we will never serve. Paul was a man who served in spite of his situation. He reported that "we dared to tell you his gospel *in spite of* strong opposition" (1 Thessalonians 2:2)—the opposition of the religious leaders, of rioters, and of imprisonment.

Another one of God's servants, Moses, had to choose to serve in spite of his situation, too. Moses was called by God to lead His people out of Egypt (Exodus 3:1-22). But there was just one problem—the people weren't sure they wanted Moses to lead them anywhere! Moses' situation was bleak.

- Moses had no credibility as a leader—he had only led sheep for 40 years.
- Moses had no authority—he came as an outsider.
- Moses had no human resources—he had only a staff.
- Moses had no help—he was later given his brother, Aaron, as an assistant.

How would you respond to this kind of commission and in this kind of situation? You and I would probably respond as Moses did, offering up a multitude of excuses about why we couldn't possibly serve.

Well, Moses finally accepted God's call to service. And he went on to lead God's people out of Egypt. Then he faithfully served God for

40 more years while the Israelites wandered in the wilderness. In the end, God called Moses "my *servant* Moses" (Numbers 12:7). Moses' circumstances weren't easy, but he passed the test. Like Paul, Moses served in spite of his situation.

## Committing to a Life of Service

Now let's fast-forward more than 3000 years to today…and to you. What is God asking you to do for Him in the way of service? Are you giving Him excuses as to why you cannot serve in your situation? Contemplate this advice from T.J. Bach, missionary to Venezuela: "If we are going to wait until every possible hindrance has been removed before we do a work for the Lord, we will never attempt to do anything."[3]

Like Paul, who served in the midst of opposition and persecution, and like Moses, who served under extreme difficulty, and like Mr. Bach, God's missionary to a foreign land, you too ought to be willing to serve your Lord, no matter what the situation. So, fill in the blank:

Yes, Lord, I am willing to serve You in spite of

_____.

There's more to learn about developing a heart for serving, and in the next chapter, we'll get to the remaining seven insights on service. But for now, think about this simple-yet-profound principle regarding impact…

*If you want to influence others,*
*you must start by serving others.*

*When you think of servanthood,*
*do you envision it as an activity*
*performed by relatively low-skilled people*
*at the bottom of the positional totem pole?*
*If you do, you have a wrong impression.*
*Servanthood is not about position or skill.*
*It's about attitude.*[1]

—JOHN MAXWELL

# Applying the Attitude of a Servant

*Whoever wants to become great among you
must be your servant...
just as the Son of Man did not come
to be served, but to serve...*
—Matthew 20:26,28

※

I've always considered myself to be a man's man. I loved and partic-ipated in sports during my high school years. I also watch my share of sporting events (and faithfully follow the Oklahoma Sooners!). So please don't think of me as strange when I say I also have an interest in poetry. Did you see the television commercial in which the wres-tler Hulk Hogan recited his poetry? Well, I'm no Hulk Hogan, but I have written a volume of rhymes for boys drawn from the book of

Proverbs.[2] And here is my attempt to paraphrase the scripture above from Matthew 20:

> Do you want to be great?
> Do you want to be grand?
> Do you want to have influence
> on those at hand?
> Then learn to be a servant
> who's humble and true,
> Doing God's will
> your whole life through.

Ah, hmmm…let's quickly move on!

Jesus' disciples had the common-but-mistaken notion that lordship equaled leadership. Being the great leaders they thought they were, James and John, two of Jesus' disciples, asked their mother(!) to petition Jesus for two seats of prominence in Jesus' future kingdom. They thought that if they could sit in seats of influence (that is, at His right and His left), they would then be great men of influence (Matthew 20:20-21). But Jesus said just the opposite is true. He said, in essence, "If you want to have influence at the highest level, be willing to serve at the lowest level" (see Matthew 20:25-28).

As Jesus pointed out, greatness (influence) comes from being willing to serve. And in 1 Thessalonians 2:1-12, Paul gave nine insights about servanthood. So far we've learned that #1) we are to serve with a higher purpose, and #2) we are to serve in spite of our situation. Let's look now at more of Paul's insights.

## Insights on Becoming a Servant

Insight #3: *Serve with integrity*—Have you ever thought about the fact that what you believe determines how you behave? Integrity, then, comes from a correct belief system. And the integrity of your service is built on a right understanding of God and His Word. That's why Paul could say to those whom he served in Thessalonica, "The appeal we make does not spring from error or impure motives" (1 Thessalonians 2:3).

The title "public servant" is often used to speak of our government officials. The men and women in public office have been elected by "we the people" and are in office to serve us. At the beginning of our country's history, public service and integrity were seen as indivisible. But sad to say, in today's society, integrity and service are no longer seen as dual requirements for government officials. There are many who serve in government without integrity.

But that's not God's standard for service. Integrity is an indispensable quality for God's servants to possess. For example, consider the character of the men who were carefully and prayerfully selected as servers in the church in Acts 6:3. They were to be "men of good reputation, full of the Spirit and of wisdom" (NASB). And what important task were they asked to do? To serve tables! Friend, you and I are to serve with integrity no matter what God asks us to do—even if it's serving tables—because we serve a holy God who demands integrity from us, His servants.

Insight #4: *Serve to please God*—Every time you and I serve, we must ask, Who am I serving? If our service is done to please men, then we are not serving God. We can't do both. Paul knew that. So he declared up front, "We speak as men approved by God...not trying to please men" (1 Thessalonians 2:4). Listen as Paul explained elsewhere:

> Am I now trying to win the approval of men, or of God?
> Or am I trying to please men? If I were still trying to please
> men, I would not be a servant of Christ (Galatians 1:10).

Aaron, the brother of Moses, was of great help during the exodus of the children of Israel and in the beginning of the trip to the Promised Land. But Aaron had a problem—he was a man-pleaser. While Moses was on Mount Sinai for 40 days receiving the Ten Commandments from God, the people became restless. They began to wonder if Moses was still alive, and asked Aaron to "make us gods who will go before us" (Exodus 32:1). Aaron immediately caved in to their request and made them a golden calf to worship (verses 2-6).

You see, Aaron had a choice. He could have resisted the demands of the people and said, "No way!" and thus he would have been serving God. Instead, he served the people and not God. Now do you see why it's vital for us to ask who we are serving?

Insight #5: *Serve with pure motives*—Whereas the previous insight dealt with pleasing men, this insight deals with pleasing ourselves. Okay, so you're not a man-pleaser. That's good! But...do you love the praise others give when you serve? Do you outwardly refuse the thanks and attention others give you while inwardly you are saying, "Keep the praise coming...give me more!"? Not so with Paul! He served with pure motives from the start: "We never used flattery, nor did we put on a mask to cover up greed...We were not looking for praise" (1 Thessalonians 2:5-6).

The Bible tells it like it is—"the heart is deceitful above all things" (Jeremiah 17:9). And Jeremiah, the writer of this truth, added that the heart is "beyond cure"! Is your service done for the praise you receive from others? Check your heart and make sure your motives are pure.

Insight #6: *Serve with love*—There is no greater example of loving service than that seen in a mother. Those of us who are married and have children have seen the loving service our wives give to our children when they are sick, when they suffer in any way or at any time. I'm sure that's why our little ones love to snuggle up against their mother. The servant attitude of love is what you and I must offer in our service as well.

And that's the attitude with which Paul served others. He put it this way: "We were gentle among you, like a mother...We loved you... we were delighted to share...our lives as well...because you had become so dear to us" (1 Thessalonians 2:7-8). Love is a fruit of the Spirit (Galatians 5:22), and it is Spirit-empowered love that will energize your service anywhere it is needed. (And, don't forget that attitude of love starts right in your own home with your self-sacrificing love for your beautiful wife and the best-looking kids on the block!)

Insight #7: *Serve sacrificially*—By definition, a servant sacrifices for the needs of the ones he serves. How much are you willing to give in your service for the needs of others? Paul said he was willing to work night and day to serve. He wrote, "Surely you remember, brothers, our toil and hardship; we worked night and day in order not to be a burden to anyone" (1 Thessalonians 2:9). Do you have that kind of attitude when you are asked to serve? Do you serve sacrificially?

As I was writing this, I thought of another man who served others sacrificially. We don't even know his name, but we do know of his sacrificial deeds. His story was told by Jesus in Luke 10:30-37. We call him the Good Samaritan. Let me list his deeds of sacrificial service on behalf of a complete stranger:

- He sacrificed time by stopping to help a wounded man (verse 33).

- He sacrificed his possessions by bandaging and dressing the man's wounds (verse 34).

- He sacrificed his personal transportation by carrying the man to an inn (verse 34).

- He sacrificed his life by personally taking care of the man (verse 34).

- He sacrificed his money by giving a day's wages and a blank check to an innkeeper as an advance payment for the continued care of the wounded man (verse 35).

This, brother, is what it means to serve sacrificially. Do you think the Samaritan had an impact on the wounded man? He saved the man's life by stopping to help, for a start. The Bible doesn't say what further contact he might have had with the injured man, but we can only imagine the impact!

As you read through the story of the Good Samaritan, you will also notice two other men mentioned—a priest and a Levite. They, too, saw the wounded man...and walked by on the other side of the road. They had no contact with the man in need (verses 31-32). Therefore they had no impact, and obviously, no influence. I think you will agree with me, as this story so graphically illustrates, that *the greater the sacrifice one makes, the greater the influence one can make.*

Insight #8: *Serve blamelessly*—This insight into the heart of Paul takes us back to Insight #3, *serve with integrity.* Paul wrote, "You are witnesses, and so is God, of how holy, righteous and blameless we were among you" (1 Thessalonians 2:10). The word "blameless" means that no one can bring a charge against you. You are a "Teflon Christian"—no accusation can stick to you. Again, do you think God wants His servants to be pure? I think you know the answer—*yes*! That's why God requires that His servant-leaders be "above reproach" (1 Timothy 3:2) and "blameless" (Titus 1:6). And God requires this same standard for you and me as well. When you and I strive to have a life that is pure, our service will take on a blameless quality. Our service will be motivated by the desire to please God and selflessly assist others.

Insight #9: *Serve to nurture*—Do you realize that even if you say nothing to those you serve, you are still teaching volumes? You nurture others by your Christlike example of selfless service. Paul did this. He explained, "We dealt with each of you as a father deals with his own children, encouraging, comforting and urging you to live lives worthy of God" (1 Thessalonians 2:11-12). What wife wouldn't be built up and encouraged by a husband who loved her with the kind of sacrificial service Paul showed to the Thessalonians, or Christ showed to His disciples? What child wouldn't be motivated and inspired to follow Christ after having seen Christ's love demonstrated and modeled by his or her father? On and on it goes. Our nurturing service to others at home, at church, or on the job—providing help, encouragement, and hope—will hopefully point others toward God and godly behavior.

That is quite a list, isn't it? Paul's comments about his brief time—a mere three weeks!—with the people of Thessalonica have given us nine great insights into what it means to have a heart for service. But given that Paul was with these people for such a short period of time, are you wondering whether Paul could possibly have had an effect on them?

Be sure and read the entire account for yourself in 1 Thessalonians 1:5-9. Here's a brief summary of the impact of Paul's heart for serving the Thessalonians:

> They became converts.
> They became imitators of Paul's life.
> They became imitators of the Lord.
> They became models to others.
> They became messengers of the gospel to all.

Paul's influence was felt, even though his visit was so short. Not only did Paul have an impact on these people, but these people, in turn, went on to have an impact upon others. Paul's influence was felt for hundreds of miles through the impact he made on this one group of people as they went about modeling Paul's heart for serving. Let's never be guilty of underestimating the power of a man with a servant's attitude!

## Getting Started on a Life of Servanthood

I hope that by now you are seeing how you can impact others by having a servant's attitude and that you are asking, "Where do I start?" Let me offer you a few tips on how to get started on the road to servanthood.

*Servanthood is not natural*—Start by praying that God would work in your heart. No man is the servant he *could* be. Ask God to make you the servant you should be.

*Servanthood is not an office, but a ministry*—Start by serving with humility. True influence always takes the posture of a servant.

*Servanthood begins at home*—Start by serving those who live under your own roof—your wife and children. What you are at home is what you are!

*Servanthood is a lifestyle*—Start by taking every opportunity to serve others at all times. A servant is not on part-time duty. He is fully committed with the whole of his being.

*Servanthood has no selfish motives*—Start by sacrificing your time, your money, and your energy for the needs of others. A servant gives, asking for nothing in return.

*Servanthood is our calling*—Start by acting like a servant. A servant is one who has been given this task by his Master. Own it!

*Servanthood requires no training*—Start today! You don't need to wait for a class called Servanthood 101 to learn how to serve. No excuses can or should be given. What are you waiting for?

## The Impact of a Servant

Serving others does have an influential effect on others. We saw this in the service of Jesus, D.L. Moody, the apostle Paul, and Stan Miller.

At the beginning of chapter 18, I related the story of one man who, all life long, selfishly took from others and basically had little or no impact. If he had any influence at all, it was negative.

On the other hand, my friend Stan Miller spent his whole life serving his family and anyone else who crossed his path. His godly influence was and will be felt for generations to come.

Now, my friend, which one of these men will you pattern your life after? Will you serve, or insist on being served? The choice is yours. And remember...

*The greater the level of*
*your service to others,*
*the greater the level of*
*your impact on others.*

*Key #9*

# Excellence

*The standard for excellence—the character of God*
*The motivation for excellence—the glory of God*
*The direction of excellence—the will of God*
*The focus of excellence—godly character*
*The picture of excellence—servanthood*
*The cost of excellence—discipleship*[1]
—GARY INRIG

# Cultivating Excellence

*Whatever you do, whether in word or deed,*
*do it all in the name of the Lord Jesus.*
—Colossians 3:17

☙❧

The captain of the plane came on the intercom with a cheery voice and announced that we were fifteenth in line to takeoff. Having already put everything away in preparation for takeoff, Elizabeth and I sat in our plane seats with nothing to work on. If your job requires you to fly often, you know having nothing to do is an unpardonable sin. Plane time is work time!

So as we sat there on the runway at O'Hare Airport in Chicago, we began looking at the *Sky Mall* catalog that's placed in every seat pocket. (As you can tell, we were pretty desperate for something to do!) In the catalog we noticed a unique collection of CDs entitled "The World's

100 Greatest People." Can you imagine the honor it would be to end up on the list of the 100 greatest people out of the billions who have ever lived on this earth?

*Who were these people?* we wondered. *And what made their influence so great? What had they done to become part of such an exclusive list?*

These questions were so compelling that I pulled out the telephone provided for plane passengers and phoned the toll-free number to order the set. As I hung up the phone, the captain came on the speaker and said we were making good progress...now there were only ten planes ahead of us!

## The Definition of Excellence

With my questions continuing to bounce around in my head, the CDs finally arrived. I tore into the box and began to listen and learn about these people of influence, people who made a positive contribution, people who made a difference. In short, people with "Achieving Personalities," as they were described on the back cover of the storage box. Soon I noticed a single, shiny golden thread that was woven throughout the lives of these greats—every one of them had cultivated excellence in their areas of greatness. Their lives of influence and accomplishment radiated a desire to do their best in their field of endeavor.

That's what excellence means—doing your best. Which brings us to our next key: The man who makes a difference—a man of impact—is committed to a life of excellence.

Many of "the world's 100 greatest people" were committed to excellence because they saw their life as a stewardship. And that should be our focus as well. Consider this definition of excellence:

> Excellence is the maximum exercise of one's gifts and abilities within the range of responsibilities given by God.[2]

This is an excellent definition, for it keeps in mind that God is the one who determines the standard of excellence for us. The measure of excellence is unique for each of us because God has given you and me different sets of talents and abilities. And He expects us to be good stewards of these resources.

## The Illustration of Excellence

Is it any wonder that Paul was included on the list of the world's 100 greatest people included in my boxed CD set? Let's look at Paul's life and see what made him a man of impact. And by God's grace, maybe we can follow in his footsteps.

*Paul's ministry at Thessalonica*—How long does it take for your life to impact another person? Sometimes it's only one meeting, or a few contacts. But usually the rule is the greater the intensity and focus, the greater will be the impact. It goes without saying that Paul was an intense man and, as a result, everywhere he went his impact was felt. He made a definite difference in people's lives.

Paul's public ministry at Thessalonica occurred over a period of only three Sabbaths (Acts 17:2), and his total time there was fairly brief— maybe no more than four to six months. But the difference he made was monumental! He later wrote to this new church and declared that their testimony throughout the region was so powerful that he and his traveling companions didn't need to say anything. Believers from Thessalonica had already been all over the region with the gospel. Why was Paul's impact on the Thessalonians so great? Here are some clues:

Paul's ministry was more than a job—he gave out the good news of the gospel, and he also gave of himself (1 Thessalonians 2:8).

Paul's ministry was not a financial burden to others—he labored night and day to support himself and preached when he was able to (verse 9).

Paul's behavior was blameless (verse 10).

Paul's message was personally offered "as a father deals with his own children" (verse 11).

What a great description of excellence! Paul did his job to the best of his ability, sacrificing of himself and using whatever resources were at his disposal. As a result, a town and a region were significantly impacted for Jesus Christ.

*Paul's ministry at Ephesus*—On his third missionary journey, Paul arrived at Ephesus, a major city on the western coast of what is now Turkey. He stayed there for three years, preaching and teaching (Acts 19). His ministry was so effective that the makers of idols for the local temples united and started a riot, forcing Paul to leave town. After a brief ministry in Greece, he made his way back to Miletus, located 30 miles from Ephesus. Because Paul had not been able to say his goodbyes to the church leaders in Ephesus, he asked them to meet him at Miletus. The passage that describes his meeting with these elders and his messages to them gives us even more glimpses of how Paul ministered with excellence (Acts 20:17-38).

- Paul's ministry was not restricted—"You know that I have not hesitated to preach anything that would be helpful to you but have taught you publicly and from house to house" (verse 20).

- Paul's ministry was thorough—"I have not hesitated to proclaim to you the whole will of God" (verse 27).

- Paul's ministry was passionate—"So be on your guard! Remember that for three years I never stopped warning each of you night and day with tears" (verse 31).

- Paul's ministry was unselfish—"I have not coveted anyone's silver or gold or clothing. You yourselves know that these hands of mine have supplied my own needs and the needs of my companions" (verses 33-34).

In Paul we see the work ethic and spiritual power of a man who models excellence for others. What sort of impact did Paul have on these men and the members of the church at Ephesus?

When he had said this, he knelt down with all of them and prayed. They all wept as they embraced him and kissed him. What grieved them most was his statement that they would never see his face again. Then they accompanied him to the ship (verses 37-38).

## The Description of Excellence

Paul saw his life and his spiritual gifts, abilities, and education as a stewardship. He explained it in these words:

> If I preach voluntarily, I have a reward; if not voluntarily, I am simply discharging the trust [stewardship] committed to me (1 Corinthians 9:17).

> Surely you have heard about the administration [stewardship] of God's grace that was given to me for you (Ephesians 3:2).

> I have become [the church's] servant by the commission [stewardship] God gave me to present to you the word of God in its fullness (Colossians 1:25).

Are you perceiving your life as a stewardship from God and an opportunity to fulfill His desires and purpose for you? I truly hope so. It's a vital key and motivator to excellence. To help us strive for excellence in our own lives, take note of the qualities that spell out E-X-C-E-L-L-E-N-C-E.

**E**—*Eyes the goal*—A man who makes a difference lives a focused and fine-tuned life. Regardless of the distractions that come his way, he concentrates on the matters that have the greatest importance. He knows and accepts that he will not be able to do all things, and certainly not do all things well. What one grand goal will your life be known for? Paul understood the need to keep his eyes fixed on the goal. He declared, "This one thing I do," not "These many things I dabble in"!

**X**—*Excels at finding solutions*—A man who makes a difference is creative. He's always thinking, always looking for answers and fresh solutions. He is flexible, innovative, and always endeavors to find a way to make things work. Are there any problems you are wrestling with today? Maybe it's time to think outside the box. That's how the man who makes a difference would approach your problem.

**C**—*Curious about the future*—A man who makes a difference is a visionary. He's a forward thinker. A planner. He plans for the future in his personal life, his ministry life, his business life, and ultimately he has planned for his future life in eternity. As a visionary he will have a powerful and permanent influence on his generation because he's able to see more and farther ahead than others. He is a man of faith, for faith is vision. What are your plans for the future? The man who makes a difference has a plan!

**E**—*Excited about change*—A man who makes a difference is flexible. He has a burning desire to know the truth and is flexible, willing to make changes in his life if they're needed. Take a look at your life. Are you stuck in a rut? It's said that the definition of a rut is that it's a grave with the ends kicked out! What are some areas of your life that you need to revisit with an eye toward change? Don't live another year doing the same old things. If you don't change, the world will change around you and you'll be left behind.

**L**—*Learns from everyone*—A man who makes a difference has a passion for learning. He has an unquenchable thirst for growing and willingly seeks out anyone who can aid his thirst. He prepares himself for any task by researching, reading, and training. A man with a spirit of learning will encounter no hurdle he cannot overcome. It's been said that continuous learning is the minimum requirement for success in any field. No matter what disadvantages a guy has experienced or what setbacks he's encountered, Henry Stanley has a personal message for him—and for us!

Henry Stanley lived in the 1800s and started his life with every disadvantage you could imagine. He was deserted by his mother when he was only two and raised in a poorhouse. Stanley could have excused himself, like many do, from any opportunity to live a life of influence. Yet with a passion for learning, he went on to become a missionary and explorer in Africa, a member of the British Parliament, and was knighted in 1899. So we've got no excuses. We too can be learners and overcomers.

**L**—*Loves to take risks*—A man who makes a difference does not settle for security and comfort. He is willing to break with convention if he believes it to be the will of God for his life.

When I lived in Singapore with my family, I had the privilege of meeting Hudson Taylor III, the great-grandson of Hudson Taylor, the founder of China Inland Mission. Hudson Taylor believed he was called by God to go to China. However, no mission board would sponsor him. So, rather than give up, he founded China Inland Mission. Because of his willingness to take a risk and strike out on his own to follow God's leading, he and hundreds of others went to China under this mission's banner and were a great influence for the cause of Christ...all because God was able to use one man who was willing to take a risk.

If you could do anything or be anything, what would it be? I'm sure that your answer would involve taking some risk on your part—like quitting your job, moving to another state, going back to school, etc. But without the risk, you will never fulfill your desires. So after much careful prayer and seeking wise counsel, if you believe it's God's will, go for it!

**E**—*Endures opposition*—A man who makes a difference is willing to endure pain, suffering, and persecution in order to accomplish God's demands on his life. He will persevere through all obstacles and opposition. We've already considered the apostle Paul's life of adversity—the prisons, the beatings, the treachery, the persecutions (2 Corinthians 11:23-27). "Yet," as it is written, "from such rocky soil grew the fruit of his ministry. Adversity builds character, perspective and vision into the life of a leader."[3]

How solid are your convictions, your desires, your determinations to be a man of impact? Your ability to withstand the pressures produced by your convictions will determine how deep-seated your convictions really are.

**N**—*Names failure as a learning experience*—A man who makes a difference has Resilience…and that's with a capital R! He's able to bounce back after what seems to be failure or a setback. He uses such experiences as learning opportunities. For him every step is a step forward. And no defeat is final. Every time I think of this quality of excellence, I think of Thomas Edison, the great inventor of the light bulb, who plowed through 10,000 tries—and failures—before he invented the incandescent lamp. Have you let anything stop you from moving forward in your life and your service to God? Name it, see it as a learning experience, step back, and try again!

**C**—*Convinced what he is doing is important*—A man who makes a difference has conviction. Anything he believes to be the will of God is entered into with the full force of his being. Therefore he can endure great difficulty and adversity in the course of completing a task. His confidence is not in his own abilities, but in God's ability to work through his limited abilities. As martyred missionary Jim Elliot exhorted, "Live to the hilt every situation you believe to be the will of God." What are the important things in your life? Begin a list of them and, with the full force of your being and the power of God behind you, move forward regardless of the opposition.

**E**—*Envisions a higher purpose*—A man who makes a difference has a sense of God's calling on his life. Whether he's a minister, a missionary, a mason, or a meter reader, he does his work as though he is doing it for the Lord (Colossians 3:23). He is compelled to live out every area of his life to the maximum—to the hilt!—for

God's glory and the good of others. Do you view your job as a calling from God? Whatever your job, resolve to make it your calling, your vocation, a calling from God.

## The Reward of Excellence

The saddest possible scenario in a man's life, in my opinion, is the one that's played out by many a man on his deathbed. Yes, there is sadness in his impending departure from this life. But what's just as sad is his confession that he wasn't all he could have been and that he didn't do all he could have done. Yes, his life had meaning. And sure, there was joy along the way. But in his heart he knows that he squandered some areas of the stewardship of his life and abilities. He knows that there was more he could have given, more he could have done.

But it doesn't have to be that way for you. Living a life of daily excellence ensures a life of lasting impact. Paul illustrated the rewards that come from being a man of excellence when he gave us his "deathbed" affirmation in 2 Timothy 4:6-8.

*Excellence leaves no regrets*—Paul saw his life as a sacrificial offering to God. All of his sacrifices had been worth the effort. He was ready to leave his earthly life without regret.

> I am already being poured out like a drink offering, and the time has come for my departure (verse 6).

*Excellence gives of its best*—Paul saw himself as a soldier who had completed his mission, or a runner who had finished the race. He saw his life as complete. With the Lord's help, he had been able to complete all that God had called him to do. He was able to declare,

> I have fought the good fight, I have finished the race (verse 7).

*Excellence defines the standard*—Paul did not fail to impart to his listeners the whole counsel of God. For him the standard of excellence was the truths of the revealed Word of God and not his own opinions.

I have kept the faith (verse 7).

*Excellence reinforces character*—Character is what you are in the dark when no one is looking. Paul demanded excellence in himself and those who served with him in ministry. He also saw a man's character as essential for leadership. Paul knew that God was his judge, and was confident that his life of excellence mirrored his character. He knew what awaited him in heaven.

> Now there is in store for me the crown of righteousness,
> which the Lord, the righteous Judge, will award to me
> on that day (verse 8).

Excellence defined Paul's life, and it marked him for greatness. That's why it is a vital quality for the man who makes a difference. Excellence—don't leave home without it! Endeavor, by God's grace, to live each day to its fullest, to live each day giving your all, to live each day with excellence.

*The quality of your life will be determined by
the depth of your commitment to excellence,
no matter what your chosen field.*
—VINCE LOMBARDI

# Winning the Battle in the Secret Life

*Therefore we do not lose heart.*
*Though outwardly we are wasting away,*
*yet inwardly we are being renewed day by day.*

—2 CORINTHIANS 4:16

❧

Do you have time for another airplane story? This one takes place at 37,000 feet over the Pacific Ocean. One of the perks that comes with lots of time logged in the air is an opportunity to upgrade your seating "when available." Well, a seat opened up on this flight and I was placed in a first-class seat next to a captain in the Navy submarine service. (Actually he was a commodore, an officer who commands a squadron of subs, which is a big deal!)

As we began talking I shared that my son-in-law, Paul, was also a submariner. I told him of Paul's lament over his latest assignment. He was to serve as the weapons officer on a boat out of Pearl Harbor. His concern was that the best department assignment, in his estimation, was that of engineer.

At this point the commodore chuckled. Evidently the same thing had happened to him in years past. He too was bummed when he had been assigned the task of weapons officer. Then he shared with me some advice he had received from another officer at the time. Back then, he too was feeling sorry for himself and his misfortune. He just knew his career was over. But in the midst of his pity party, this other officer had told him that ultimately it was his willingness to pay the price of excellence that would be the determining factor on whether he got a future promotion.

The commodore's response? He determined to be the best weapons officer in the command. He spent a lot of time behind the scenes, in secret, burning the midnight oil to make sure he was the best at his job. Obviously his desire to be the best paid off, as he was, at that time, in line for an admiral's star. I couldn't wait to get off that plane and call Paul with that same advice—*Pay the price to be the best at whatever you're doing!*

## Your Secret Life Illustrated

Several years ago my wife and I were in Alaska for a joint speaking engagement. On Saturday afternoon, while the women were finishing up their part of the conference, a commercial fisherman treated me to a trip around Petersburg Bay on his fishing boat. What a thrill! We saw sea lions, seals, eagles, and even several whales. But what inspired the greatest awe (and fear!) in me was the icebergs. The captain of the boat, exercising great caution, steered clear of them. It was obvious he too was in awe of them!

In fact, the captain made a very wide berth around one particularly large berg. As we circled the frozen mass he explained why icebergs are so feared and respected. Seven-eighths of the mass of an iceberg is below the surface. We were seeing only one-eighth of the total mass. How far out did the ice extend under the water? The captain couldn't know. All we could do was view its ominous presence with great respect…and from a great distance!

Friend, what's true about icebergs is true about your life. Your secret life, your inner life, is much like the mass of an iceberg, which is largely below the surface, away from the public eye. Just as an iceberg's strength and power comes largely from the unseen portion, it's the secret part of your life—when handled with excellence—that gives you the power to have an outward and awesome impact.

## Your Secret Life and Excellence

I hope you're already realizing how important your secret life is. I call it "the secret life" because it's the private life of a man that no one sees. The "inner man" is what the Bible calls it. And why is the quality of your secret life so vital? Because this is where life's battles are fought…and won. The inner life encompasses your mind—what you think and think on. It includes your will—what you decide you will and won't do. And it centers on your heart. As the Bible says, "as [a man] thinketh in his heart, so is he" (Proverbs 23:7 KJV).

Well, my friend, it is as a man *desires* to become a man of influence that he begins to win the battle of the secret life. And I think you can see where the problem lies—it's in the weakness of our flesh. We are basically lazy. It's easier to go with the flow. We put out just enough effort to get by. But you and I must want that vibrant inner life badly enough to pay the price necessary to achieve growth and spiritual maturity. What a blessed reward will be ours if we are willing to pay the price— we will become men who can make a difference. We will leave a positive mark on the lives of others.

## Nurturing Your Secret Life

In my book *A Man After God's Own Heart,* I share a little of my struggle with my early Christian walk and how one day I woke up realizing I needed to face the reality of my disobedience and spiritual laziness. That was the beginning of my desire to "return home" in my walk with the Lord. Since then I've endeavored to diligently, carefully, seriously, and painstakingly nurture my secret life. And it's not always been easy. In fact, it's downright hard. I've faced many struggles through the years. But by God's grace, it's been a joyous and exciting journey of growth and some measure of impact.

But enough about me. Now for you. What will godly desire and a carefully nurtured secret life produce in you? What kind of man will you become as you follow through on your desire to become someone who has a positive influence on others, someone who makes a lasting impact? What are the traits you will nurture in your inner life that will equip you to make a difference in the lives of others?

- You will develop deep personal convictions. These convictions will come from your desire to be obedient in all areas of your life to your Lord Jesus Christ.

- You will subordinate all of your life under a set of God-centered goals—goals that embrace all the major areas of a person's life.

- You will establish and maintain a personal life of discipline—understanding that spiritual discipline and physical discipline are bound as one.

- You will make wiser and more biblical decisions. Why? Because you are beginning to understand that the essence of the Christian life resides in the will.

- You will embrace the concept of influence—your godly impact on others.

- You will accept the challenge of living a godly life—a life that will have an influence on others.

- You will embrace the concept of serving others. There can be no impact without contact—contact that desires to give with no expectation.

- You will understand that to have an influence on people you must establish the right priorities in your life…and people must be one of your top priorities.
- You will sense that your life has purpose and destiny.

What a powerful force you and I can be in the hands of God! But it starts with your secret life, a life that desires excellence. So what are you going to do? Develop the secret life and expand your influence… or squander away the gift of a life meant to impact others and leave an indelible mark? I think I know your answer. A desire to cultivate your inner life will give you the edge of excellence that will separate you from the average and empower you for significance. A life of great public influence starts by nurturing a deep, private inner life.

## Determining to Become a Man of Excellence

Endeavor to live each day to its fullest, to live each day with excellence. And that, of course, is going to take commitment. As Vince Lombardi said in the quote that appears at the beginning of this chapter, "The quality of your life will be determined by the depth of your commitment to excellence, no matter what your chosen field."

So the question for you (and me) today is this: Where, what, and how deep is your commitment to excellence? In relation to any kind of commitment, one sharp writer divided people into four types:

- *Cop-outs*—People who have no goals and do not make commitments.
- *Holdouts*—People who don't know if they can reach their goals, so they're afraid to make commitments.
- *Dropouts*—People who start toward a goal but quit when the going gets tough.
- *All-outs*—People who set goals, commit to them, and pay the price to reach them.[1]

I'm sure your desire is to do well and be that man of excellence, to be an all-out man of influence who makes a lasting impact. With that desire in mind, here are some ways you can improve on making and keeping your commitments to excellence.

*Determine the areas of your life where greater commitment is needed*— How you spend your time and money are the two greatest indicators of your focus and interest. So take a look at your calendar and your checkbook and determine what you've been committing yourself to. Ask yourself if these are the right priorities for you as a Christian man. Will these pursuits increase your level of excellence? Maybe you need to readjust your priorities. If you're a workaholic, a sports fanatic, or overly materialistic, maybe you need help re-prioritizing your life. Make the things of God your first priority. As the verse for this chapter reminds us, "Whatever you do, whether in word or deed, do it all in the name of the Lord Jesus" (Colossians 3:17).

*Determine the extent of commitment that is needed*—Some areas of life call for more of a commitment than others. For instance, exercise requires commitment, but it doesn't demand the same level of commitment as your job. Ask God to help you discern the level of commitment required in the various areas of your life. Then seek excellence in the areas you commit to. That's where the influence will come from.

*Determine whether you are willing to make a higher level of commitment*—After giving thought and prayer to your priorities and the level of commitment needed in each area of your life, the next step is to determine whether you are willing to pay the price of excellence. It costs to be a growing Christian man of influence. It costs to be a man of God. It costs to be the kind of husband the Bible calls you to be. It costs to be a good parent and to be the best at work. And it costs to serve in your church. Commitment to excellence always comes at a cost!

*Determine what it will take to keep your commitments to excellence*— Ask God to help you follow through on the commitments you want to make for His glory and the good of others. And ask someone to hold you accountable to those commitments. Finally, remember that God has handed you the baton for "the race of life." Others are depending on you to keep your commitments for the long haul and to provide a model of excellence—whether it's at home, on the job, at church, or in your community. Please take care not to drop the baton that's been passed on to you. Be faithful and keep your commitments to excellence!

## Final Thoughts on the Secret Life and Excellence

My conversation with the Navy captain was insightful. And my boat trip in Alaska made for a memorable day! That trip was unforgettable. My encounter with those large icebergs left me impressed and awed. And, my friend, that's the way it can be with your life and mine…if we settle once and for all the issue of the necessity of nurturing our secret life of excellence according to God's Word. Once we make that decision and act on it, the results of our inner change will emerge above the surface to leave a breathtaking and lasting impact on others.

But I can't help but share one more experience. As I was writing about the huge icebergs in Alaska, I was looking out my window toward the east at Mount Rainier and thought of another illustration. Off in the distance, Mount Rainier towers over the Cascade Range at a prominent 14,411 feet (or 4,392 meters).

This incredible mountain illustrates how our secret life affects our outer life. Mount Rainier was created when hot molten lava was pushed from the depths beneath the earth and shot upward toward the surface. As I see it, the force of the underground pressure of our secret life pushes our inner character upward and onward until we too stand tall like the mighty Mount Rainier, jutting forth for all to behold.

Aren't these great ways to picture your life? As an awesome iceberg? Or a majestic mountain? All because you've nurtured excellence in the inner man according to God's ways.

So, brother, what do you need to faithfully nurture in your inner life that will bring excellence to your actions, whether spiritual or secular? What can you do to move yourself toward fulfilling your goals and desires? It's the extra thing, extra time, extra study, extra research, extra effort, extra desire that will result in excellence. If you want to have an impact as a teacher, or engineer, or salesman, it's what is done in secret, over and above the normal, that leads to a life of excellence.

Excellence is yet another key that results in a life of impact. The secret work of excellence will eventually give outward evidence of a life of internal vitality. What others see will be the payoff for the time and care you take with your private life with God and your endeavors to become the best you can be. These external evidences are what make us men of impact. And impact is based on character, and character is developed in secret.

### A Prayer for Excellence

Lord, I want to thank You for Your commitment in securing my salvation in Jesus Christ. I ask that You help me stay committed to the standards of Your Word. Please give me wisdom as I determine my priorities. I ask for Your Holy Spirit to strengthen my resolve to follow through on these priorities. May I accept the challenge of living a life committed to You and to excellence. From this day forward, as I seek to become a man of impact, may I be known as one who strives for excellence and the keeping of my commitments, regardless of the cost. Amen.

## TEN KEYS TO A LIFE OF IMPACT

*Key #10*

# Mentoring

*If I had my life to live over again,*
*I would live it to change the lives of people,*
*because you have not changed anything*
*until you've changed the lives of people.*[1]
—WARREN WEBSTER

# Recognizing the Importance of Mentoring

*The things you have heard me say
in the presence of many witnesses
entrust to reliable men
who will also be qualified to teach others.*

—2 TIMOTHY 2:2

The topic of mentoring has become very fashionable in recent years. Numerous books from both the business world and the church have been written on the subject of having and being a mentor.

Have you ever wondered where the concept of mentoring came from? I have…and I did a little research and discovered that the word *mentor* has an interesting history. It seems that in the eighth century B.C., the poet Homer wrote, in his major Greek work *The Odyssey,* about a man named *Mentor.* Mentor was the friend of the warrior

Odysseus. When Odysseus went off to fight in the Trojan War, Mentor was left in charge of Odysseus's household. Mentor was also charged with teaching, tutoring, and protecting Odysseus's son, Telemachus. Mentor was faithful to "mentor" Telemachus until his father returned many years later.

This, my friend, is a great illustration of the meaning of the word *mentor*. In our culture today, anyone who is an experienced advisor, supporter, teacher, coach, or tutor has taken on the title of *mentor* in the tradition of Odysseus's faithful friend, Mentor.

## The Influence of a Mentor

With my busy schedule, I don't have a lot of time for hobbies. I do a little running and sometimes pump a little iron. And I play golf once a year with my sons-in-law. Beyond that I'm a pretty busy but dull person. But one thing I enjoy doing is visiting bookstores wherever my business or ministry endeavors take me.

I prefer visiting Christian bookstores for resources related to biblical studies and spiritual growth, but I also like going into general bookstores. So whether it's one or the other, I delight in leafing through as many books as I can, looking for the right ones to purchase. My particular areas of interest are leadership, discipleship, mentoring, Bible studies, and Christian living. Over the years I have noticed a large number of books on the shelves that are dedicated to Dr. Howard Hendricks, the distinguished professor and chair of the Center for Christian Leadership at Dallas Theological Seminary.

Dr. Hendricks seems to epitomize what we want to cover in this last key (at least on my short list) for the man who makes a difference. I'm sure you've already guessed that the man who makes an impact has a passion for mentoring men. "Howie" Hendricks (as many of his friends call him) has taught, trained, and influenced hundreds of men at the seminary where he has taught for more than 50 years. Howie's men have graduated and become men of influence all over the world. Over the years, these men have modeled their mentor and passed on to others what Dr. Hendricks passed on to them.

In fact, right now I am holding in my hand a book on excellence. And guess what? The foreword was written by Howard D. Hendricks. This book in my hand, along with a myriad of other books and a myriad of men, speaks to the fact that Dr. Hendricks is living out the apostle Paul's exhortation to Timothy, his young protégé, to train the generations to come: "The things you have heard me say in the presence of many witnesses entrust to reliable men who will also be qualified to teach others" (2 Timothy 2:2).

## The Example of a Mentor

Long before the word *mentor* became trendy, the apostle Paul, like Mentor, was a teacher and tutor. But, unlike Mentor, who trained only one young boy, Paul was an advisor and trainer of many. Paul supported, taught, and tutored a host of men during his 20-plus years of ministry. I believe Paul was able to utter the now-famous words at the end of his life—"I have finished the race"—partly because he passed on to others what had been given to him (2 Timothy 4:7). He told the leaders at Ephesus, "I have not hesitated to proclaim to you the whole will of God" (Acts 20:27). Paul held nothing back from anyone who cared to learn from him. He passed on all that he knew. He gave his all.

The Bible doesn't record how or when Paul's life ended. Maybe that's because, in a sense, Paul's life didn't end. The famous preacher John Wesley was often quoted as saying, "God buries His workmen, but His work goes on." Well, God buried His servant Paul, but Paul's mentoring influence continued on through the following people:

*The young man Timothy*—Timothy is probably the most well known of Paul's pupils. Paul had worked with Timothy for 15 years and, at the end of Paul's days on this earth, Timothy had matured and was pastoring the flagship church at Ephesus in Asia Minor. Paul's teaching would live on in the life and ministry of Timothy as Timothy fulfilled another of Paul's exhortations: "Join with others in following my example... [and] live according to the pattern we gave you" (Philippians 3:17).

*The young man Titus*—Titus was another young man mentored

by Paul. As with Timothy, Paul entrusted Titus with more and more responsibility as he matured in the faith. Titus was the one commissioned by Paul to choose and train up leaders on the island of Crete (see the book of Titus). Because of his valuable mentoring, Paul's legacy and teaching continued to live on through the life and ministry of Titus.

*The lives of others*—Besides Timothy and Titus, there were a multitude of others who were deeply influenced by Paul. For instance…

*Paul developed disciples from the very beginning of his ministry* (in Damascus), and these disciples helped Paul escape from his enemies (Acts 9:25). Paul's influence lived on in the lives of these faithful and fearless followers.

*Paul developed disciples during his first missionary journey.* Many of these men would stay with him even in the midst of much persecution (Acts 14:19-20). In spite of difficult situations, Paul's influence lived on in the lives of these courageous disciples.

*Paul developed disciples during his time in Ephesus.* In fact, the Ephesian elders evidenced their devotion to Paul by traveling over 40 hours to spend just a few hours with their beloved mentor as he passed nearby on his way to Jerusalem (Acts 20:17-18). When Paul left Ephesus, "he knelt down with all of them and prayed. They all wept as they embraced him and kissed him…Then they accompanied him to the ship" (Acts 20:36-38). Paul's influence would most definitely live on in the lives of these devoted and grateful men.

*Paul developed disciples in Corinth.* Paul lived and worked with a husband and wife named Priscilla and Aquila, who became a force for Christianity. We first meet this remarkable couple in Acts 18:2. They were tentmakers and met and became friends with Paul, a fellow tentmaker, in Corinth. When Paul left Corinth, they went with him. They were mentioned in Paul's letters as providing a meeting place for a church in their homes in Ephesus and later in Rome. And according to Romans 16:3-5, they "risked their lives" for Paul and the ministry.

This again shows the effect of Paul's life on others. Talk about influence! This ordinary couple did extraordinary feats because of Paul's impact on their lives. It's obvious that Paul's contact with them ensured that their lives were never the same again.

## The Greatest Mentor of All

And now let's consider the discipleship and mentoring ministry of the greatest mentor of all, Jesus Christ. (That is another whole book in itself!) Without a doubt, Jesus was the greatest mentor of all time. He set the pattern for *everyone* to follow! He took a ragtag group of a dozen uneducated, ill-equipped men and, in three years, molded them into a force that turned the religious world of their day literally upside down. Now that's influence! How did He, the greatest mentor of all, do it?

In his remarkable book *The Master Plan of Evangelism,* Robert Coleman describes Jesus' process for making disciples. I personally have become Mr. Coleman's disciple by reading his book many times, and now I offer my summary of eight points Coleman makes about Jesus' process.[2]

1. Selection—Jesus prayerfully selected 12 men. We'll take a closer look at the process of selecting disciples in the next chapter, but for now consider this: Even though Jesus was God in human flesh and He knew the hearts of all men, He spent a full night in prayer to His Father before He selected the 12 disciples. The selection process is a lot easier for you if you already have a family. In fact, you haven't selected them. God has, by assigning you to your position as husband and father, selected you to guide and disciple your family.

2. Association—Jesus spent time with His men. After He selected them, He focused much of His three-year ministry almost exclusively on them. There could be no impact without contact. Jesus wanted His men to know Him and experience His love for them. Likewise, you are to associate with your family or anyone else you are called to mentor.

3. Consecration—Jesus required obedience. You can't give water

to a man whose cup is already full. Likewise, you can't disciple a man who thinks he has all the answers. Jesus looked for men who were willing to learn—men who didn't offer excuses, but were ready and willing to obey their Master. Maybe that's why Jesus took so long before He selected his men. He was looking for men with a teachable spirit.

Before you can be a teacher of others, you must first be a learner. Discipleship starts with your willingness to obey the Master's teachings. Are you ready to listen, learn, and obey?

4. Impartation—Jesus gave Himself away, even His own life. Is it any wonder that the 12 disciples were willing to go to the ends of the earth to tell others about the One who loved them and died for their sins?

5. Demonstration—Jesus modeled godly living. He was the "Word made flesh" (see John 1:14). Every word out of His mouth was the breath of God. Every action was God's reaction to life. At the end of his Gospel, John testifies that he wrote only a portion of what Jesus had done. John said, "Jesus did many other things as well. If every one of them were written down, I suppose that even the whole world would not have room for the books that would be written" (John 21:25). Jesus' example was a powerful tool that shaped the lives of the disciples. Your example, too, is a powerful tool that can shape the lives of your family. Make sure your family sees Jesus in your life and in your responses to life.

6. Delegation—Jesus assigned work for His disciples to do. You may have heard the saying, "Give a man a fish and he can live for a day, but teach a man how to fish and he can live for a lifetime." Jesus not only modeled how to live, He also taught and sent His disciples out to show others. Responsibility is as much caught as taught. Jesus imparted His message to His men and when they were ready, He sent them out to pass that same message on to others. When it was finally time, Jesus delegated His work to the 12—and to you and me today: "Go and make disciples of all nations, baptizing them in the name of the Father and of the Son and of the Holy Spirit, and teaching them

to obey everything I have commanded you. And surely I am with you always, to the very end of the age" (Matthew 28:19-20).

7. Supervision—Jesus monitored the progress of His men. Unsupervised delegation can be a dangerous thing, especially during the early stages of training. Is the delegated task being done correctly? Jesus sent the disciples out for a specified period of time, and "when the apostles returned, they reported to Jesus what they had done. Then he took them with him and they withdrew by themselves to a town called Bethsaida" (Luke 9:1,10). Jesus followed their progress.

8. Reproduction—Jesus expected His disciples to make disciples. Discipleship or mentoring is not for the purpose of filling a file cabinet with notes and reports that are never internalized or passed on. Just as physical reproduction has as its objective the continuation of a species, so mentoring has as its objective the continuation of a body of information or a philosophy or, in our case, the reality of the risen Savior, Jesus Christ.

## Your Influence As a Mentor

As you can see from the lives of men like Paul and Howard Hendricks—and, of course, our Lord—significant influence and lasting impact requires an investment of time and concern for the lives of others. Again, you cannot have significant impact without significant contact. The closer you get to another person, the more influence you will have on that person's life.

So I must now ask the tough questions. Who are you getting close to? Who are you pouring your life into? Will you be able to say, "I have finished the race" because you have equipped others to carry on your philosophy, your life, your ministry, your influence? Are there others who have been so personally impacted by your life that, long after you are gone, your ideals, principles, and vision will live on? These are difficult but important questions to ask, questions we both need to ask ourselves before it's too late to have an impact on others.

## Developing a Passion for Mentoring

When I first arrived at the church where my family spent our 30 years as a Christian family, I was an immature believer. I didn't have a clue about what God was asking of me as a husband, father, provider, church member, or witness.

So what did I do to get help? I began by looking around the church for men who were mature in the areas in which I was weak. Then I asked them to mentor me. Some of these men were younger than me, but that didn't matter. They were much farther along on the road to maturity than I was. They had what I needed!

As I matured in my faith and in my understanding of my roles, I began to sense the responsibility I had to pass on to others what I had been taught. As I grew, the passion to help others grew. Today, more than 30 years later, I receive scores of e-mails, phone calls, or letters a week from men who tell me I have influenced their lives. When I say that, I'm not bragging—far from it. I only wish I could have given them more than I did. And I also wish I had awakened sooner to the opportunities I have had for being a man of influence.

O man of God, start growing! And as you grow, God will give *you* the same passion men like Jesus, Paul, and Howard Hendricks have displayed for mentoring other men of God. Then, as the title of the next chapter says, yours will be *a lasting impact—an impact for life!*

*God will one day bury you, His workman.*
*Your physical life will come to an end.*
*But your influence will not end.*
*God's workman will be gone, but*
*God's work will go on.*
—JIM GEORGE

# Leaving a Lasting Legacy

*Whatever you have learned or received or
heard from me, or seen in me—
put it into practice.*

—Philippians 4:9

ॐ

On one of my visits to India, my friend Chris Williams, who is definitely a man of influence, took me to visit a retiring missionary. The missionary was in the midst of selling all of his equipment before he returned home. As we chatted, I asked the man, "Where are your men? Where are the men you've mentored and trained to take over your work now that you are retiring?"

Well, I must say I wasn't prepared for this older man's answer. There were none! He had no disciples. He had trained no one. This godly man and his family had sacrificed much over their 25 years of living and ministering in this severely impoverished country. Humanly speaking, all of that sacrifice would soon be visibly gone. Why? Because there were no disciples left behind to carry on the ministry. There would be no lasting influence through the lives of others.

## Becoming Alert to Your Opportunities

What a wake-up call that was for me! And I hope it is to you as well. Brother, don't let your life slip away without personally and purposefully and positively influencing others. You have so much to give! And all through this book, you've learned how you can give—of yourself to God in obedience and discipline, of yourself in your own life and to others by setting the right goals, and of yourself to others by using your spiritual gifts and having a servant's heart. In all these ways, you can make sure that you leave a legacy to...

*Your wife*—If you are married, you have one of the greatest of all opportunities—that of leaving a lasting influence on the person who is the closest to you physically, emotionally, and spiritually, your wife. Make sure that before you die (keep in mind that insurance company statistics show that you will probably die before your wife does), you pass on a godly influence to your wife.

Dear brother, you must impart to your sweet and faithful wife a strong spiritual foundation so that she is better equipped to handle whatever the future holds. That means you must be a strong spiritual leader yourself. Don't leave behind only personal memories, as wonderful as they are. Memories fade with time. And don't leave behind only financial security. Money will take care of the physical needs, and that's important. But beyond these "things," seek to leave behind something greater—far greater! Leave behind a tower of spiritual strength that is being built now, today, through your godly example. Leave behind something that has true and lasting influence!

And yet, there is an even greater legacy than a wife who carries on your faith, your priorities, your principles, and your vision. There are...

*Your children*—Perhaps the greatest legacy you can leave behind is another godly generation. Humanly speaking, Christianity is only one generation away from extinction. Who will serve as a witness to the next generation? *You! You* are to pass on to your children the truth about Christ and Christian living. Your faith ought to become their faith. Now, we all know that we cannot grant salvation to our children. We cannot give them eternal life. No, that's God's job. But you and I can provide the right kind of godly influence in the home that will point our children to the Savior. The reality of Jesus Christ must first be evident in your life and my life before we can point our children to that same reality.

Now, I must warn you, if you haven't already found this out, your children may resist your Christian focus. They may object to your Christian standards. They may complain of your direction for their lives. But don't give in. There is a war going on for their souls and for their purity, just as there is a war going on for your soul and your purity. Do your part to provide a godly influence, and trust God to do the rest.

*Your fellow Christians*—Maybe you are reading this book and you don't have a family. Well, my friend, we all have an opportunity to influence our fellow believers, both now and in the future. Like Paul and like Timothy and Titus, you have the opportunity to spend your life mentoring others. You can make 2 Timothy 2:2 one of your life verses: "The things you have heard me say...entrust to reliable men who will also be qualified to teach others."

Whether or not we have a family, we are all called to mentor other believers at church. We are to actively look for those whom we can bring along in the faith. We, like Paul, need to be about the business of coming alongside a Timothy or a Titus and overseeing their growth in maturity and watching them flourish in their usefulness to the church. How, you ask, can you be this kind of mentor in your church?

- First, (as I've said before) you must be growing in your own faith. You cannot impart to others what you do not possess yourself.

- Second, understand and develop your spiritual gifts. As we learned earlier, God has given you special spiritual abilities for the purpose of serving others and building up your local church. Reading and studying what the Bible says about spiritual gifts will help you get a grasp of these important God-given tools (see Romans 12:4-8; 1 Corinthians 12:1-31; 1 Peter 4:10-11). With God's gifts, you can impact the lives of other Christians. Don't neglect to discover, develop, and use your gifts.

- Third, look for men who want to grow in their faith. I have often heard it put this way: "Look for *fat* men." This is not a reference to waist size. No, it's talking about...

**F**-aithful—Look for faithful men. Look for men who are where they are supposed to be, when they are supposed to be there. Look for men you can count on to do what they say they will do. Faithfulness is difficult to find, but it is an indispensable quality.

**A**-vailable—Look for men who are available. Look for men who are willing to give of their time in order to be trained and equipped for life and ministry. God is not looking solely for ability—He is looking for availability! And so should you.

**T**-eachable—Look for teachable men. Look for men who want to learn...and more specifically, men who want to learn from you. You might be thinking, *But...what can I offer to another man? What do I have that another man might benefit from?* Well, for one thing, you have read this book. You now know more than someone else knows. There are study questions in the back of the book, so take another man through this book and discuss the questions as you go through it together. Find other men and teach them what you know.

And there is yet another area where your influence is needed…

*Your world*—Many people in your life have little or no contact with a Christian other than you. They may see a "Christian" on television or read about Christians in the paper (usually in a negative light), or watch them in their neighborhood going off to church in their Sunday best. But they will seldom meet one up close and personal other than you. It's been said in a poem that "you are a living Bible, known and read by men." The clever rhyme goes on to ask, "What does the Bible say, 'according to you'?"

So, what kind of influence are you in your neighborhood? Are you exhibiting a proper representation of Christianity? And how about your behavior at work? Are you kind, thoughtful, friendly? Are you willing to help others succeed, even at your own expense? Are you going about the business of mentoring others on the job to help make your company more effective and productive? How are your relationships with your subordinates? Are you developing them, or are you using them? Just what does the Bible say, according to you?

## Leaving a Lasting Legacy

Well, my friend, we have come a long way in learning about how to become God's man of influence. We've learned from the lives of Christ Himself, the Master Discipler…the apostle Paul…the influential Howard Hendricks…and others. And now, the baton is being passed on to you. Do you want to have a lasting influence? I'm sure that like me, you want your life to be marked by positive, solid, biblical, and Christ-honoring qualities that can be passed on to others. If so, then here are some suggestions on how your influence can be felt now and for generations to come.

- Be a consistent, godly example. Start in your home.
- Be growing in your faith. God is not asking for perfection—just progression. Grow toward maturity, and pass on to others what you learn.

- Be growing in your job skills. God is asking you to work as if you were working for Him (Colossians 3:23).
- Be aware of your influence on others. Make sure it is a positive influence.
- Be available. Whether at home, at church, or on the job, others need your personal involvement in their lives.
- Be mentoring. Not only should you be available, but you should be actively training others.
- Be faithful, and then you will...
- Be fulfilled!

Dear friend, God will one day bury you, His workman, just as He buried His servant and workman Paul. Your physical life will come to an end. But your influence will not end. No, as you are faithful to pour your life into your family, your friends, your fellow workmates, and into fellow believers at church, your influence will live on through the lives of those whom you have served during your life. God's workman will be gone, but God's work will go on. You, His messenger and mentor, will be gone, but God's message will continue on. May your life and influence live on. May yours be a life of lasting impact.

*Live on, my friend. Live on!*

## Study Questions

*Chapter 1—Profiling the Man Who Makes a Difference*
Read through the list of qualities that made Paul an influential man (see page 11). In what two or three areas do you feel you're making good progress? In which areas do you need to pay more attention?

Think about Paul's appearance, his age, and the adversities he suffered. Can you relate to any of them? How does Paul's dedication—in spite of what are often considered hindrances—encourage you to get into the race, stay in the race, and keep on keeping on?

Can you think of any recent obstacles or setbacks that, in hindsight, you realized the Lord was using for your spiritual growth? In what ways have you seen the Lord show His faithfulness to you when the going gets tough?

What one truth from this chapter had the greatest impact on you, and why? After you identify the "one truth" from this chapter, record it on the "One Truth List" at the back of this book on pages 256-57.

### Chapter 2—Taking the First Step

When Paul became a Christian, the change in his life was dramatic. What things changed in your life when you received Christ as your Savior and Lord?

Read again the lists of "before and after" truths about a person's life before Christ (page 23) and after Christ (page 24). In what ways do these changes encourage you or humble you?

We cannot have a godly influence on others through our own human efforts. Jesus said, "I am the vine; you are the branches. If a man remains in me and I in him, he will bear much fruit; *apart from me you can do nothing*" (John 15:5). What does this tell you about your need to "remain in Christ"?

What one truth from this chapter had the greatest impact on you, and why? Write this on the "One Truth List" on pages 256-57.

## Key #1—The Bible

### *Chapter 3—Pursuing a Love for God's Word*

Describe your current relationship with the Bible. In what ways would you like to see it grow?

On pages 34-35, we read what David says the Bible does for us. Read through the list. Which two or three benefits from the Bible are particularly meaningful to you, and why?

Read 2 Timothy 3:16-17. What is the Bible useful for? What are some practical ways we can allow the Bible to "shape us" toward spiritual maturity?

A man who makes a difference is a man who loves God's Word. What do you need to do to cultivate a true love for the Bible? Whatever your answer, commit to making it happen!

What one truth from this chapter had the greatest impact on you, and why? Add this to your "One Truth List."

*Chapter 4—Persevering for Life*

God's Word is alive and a force of change in our lives. What one or two specific examples can you give of how the Bible has influenced your thoughts, words, or actions?

Review the four keys to the promise God gave in Joshua 1:8-9. Which of these four keys are you actively carrying out in your life now? In which keys do you see room for improvement, and how can you make that happen?

On pages 46-47 is a list of ways the Bible changes us. Can you give an example of how the Bible has...

given you wisdom (Proverbs 4:11)?

given you peace (Proverbs 3:1-2)?

kept you from sin (Psalm 119:11)?

God won't force spiritual growth on you. You must desire it enough to do something about it. What change or changes will you commit to right now to make growth happen?

What one truth from this chapter had the greatest impact on you, and why? Add this to your "One Truth List."

## Key #2—Prayer

### *Chapter 5—Understanding the Significance of Prayer*

One reason prayer is important is we use it to seek God's will for our lives. How often do you approach God in prayer before making a decision? Do you think any decision is too small to bring before the Lord? Why or why not?

What two helps do we have for making sure we don't misinterpret God when we pray?

Review the list of reasons people don't pray more often. Are there any that are true about you? What do you need to do to overcome those hindrances?

What one truth from this chapter had the greatest impact on you, and why? Add this to your "One Truth List."

*Chapter 6—Participating in a Life of Prayer*

Often we'll say we're too busy to pray. But why does it make sense for prayer to be even *more* necessary when we're busy?

Read James 1:5. What are some areas in which you need wisdom right now? List them here, and take time now to lift your request up to the Lord.

Read the list of ways Paul prayed for others (see page 67). What are some ways you can pray for your pastor? Fellow believers in your church? Members of your family?

What goal would you like to set right now for improving your prayer life? Write it here, and commit yourself to carrying it out daily.

What one truth from this chapter had the greatest impact on you, and why? Add this to your "One Truth List."

## Key #3—Obedience

*Chapter 7—Living a Life of Obedience*

Can you think of a fairly recent time when the cost of obeying God was high? Describe the situation, the choices before you, and what happened.

When there are areas of disobedience in our lives, we prevent God from using us to the fullest. What makes us reluctant to give up our disobedience? Ultimately, no matter what the situation, why is obedience always the best choice?

Sometimes when God calls us to obey, we wrongly respond, "But Lord, You don't understand." According to Proverbs 3:5-6, what is a right response?

Ananias became a man of influence because he was…

> available
> willing
> prepared

How are you doing in those three areas? How can you improve?

What one truth from this chapter had the greatest impact on you, and why? Add this to your "One Truth List."

### Chapter 8—*Following the Path of Obedience*

Review how the path of obedience can lead you to the unexpected, to clarification, and to confidence as you listen to God and make one decision at a time (as happened with the apostle Paul and his mission team). What new truths did you learn about obedience as you read about Paul's example?

Name a decision you must make. How can "the four C's" help you, and how will you put them to use as you endeavor to make the right decision?

We sometimes find ourselves filled with regret when we *disobey* God. Do you think you would ever experience regret when you *obey* God? Why not?

What one truth from this chapter had the greatest impact on you, and why? Add this to your "One Truth List."

## Key #4—Challenges

*Chapter 9—Mastering Life's Challenges*

What are some challenges you face in your pursuit to obey God? Why is living the Christian life such a challenge at times?

The influential preacher D.L. Moody said, "I never met a useful Christian who was not a student of the Bible." Why should we expect a correlation between our knowledge of the Bible and our usefulness to God?

Review the practical steps to mastering the challenges of the flesh (see page 98). Which of these suggestions do you find real helpful now, and why?

What one truth from this chapter had the greatest impact on you, and why? Add this to your "One Truth List."

*Chapter 10—Accepting the Challenge to Live Boldly*

In this chapter we looked at three common areas of challenge to obedience: the challenge of fear, the challenge of peer pressure, and the challenge of culture. In which of these have you recently experienced challenges? What have you found helpful for overcoming those challenges?

List the five steps for living a strong, bold life of influence. Which steps have you benefited from in the past, and how? Which step are you eager to work on more?

Read 2 Corinthians 12:8. What encouragement do you receive from this promise?

What one truth from this chapter had the greatest impact on you, and why? Add this truth to your "One Truth List" on page 257.

## Key #5—Discipline

*Chapter 11—Pursuing Spiritual Discipline*

What qualities do the best athletes generally share that makes them excel at what they do? Which of those qualities do you perceive would be good to cultivate in the Christian life? List them here.

One characteristic of spiritual discipline is that it's demanding. If you were to compare your "spiritual workout" to getting in shape physically, how would you rate? What are the benefits of submitting yourself to a demanding regimen in terms of your spiritual growth?

"If you and I are God's children, then we should want to be like God as much as is humanly possible." In what ways does your life point other people to God? In what ways could you improve in this area?

What one truth from this chapter had the greatest impact on you, and why? Add this truth to your "One Truth List."

## Chapter 12—Practicing Personal Discipline

List here the five steps toward a more disciplined life. Which one or two steps stand out the most to you, and why?

You may have heard it said that every journey begins with a single step. What first step would you like to take now toward practicing better personal discipline?

Read the list titled "The Nature of Discipline" on page 130. Mark two or three items that, if practiced by you, would cause your life to become more disciplined. What will you do about them...and when?

What one truth from this chapter had the greatest impact on you, and why? Add this truth to your "One Truth List."

## Key #6—Goals

*Chapter 13—Developing Lifelong Goals*

Have you written down any of your life goals? If yes, review them now. How are you doing? And if no, get your calendar and schedule a time to think over and develop your lifetime goals. List them as simply and clearly as possible on a sheet of paper.

List here the benefits of having goals, as stated on pages 135-37. Which benefit would help you the most right now, and why?

In the chapter we looked at eight areas of life that call for goals. How are you doing in the five ways you can exercise yourself toward greater spiritual growth? (see page 138). Briefly share how you would benefit from each one of these "exercises."

What one truth from this chapter had the greatest impact on you, and why? Add this truth to your "One Truth List."

*Chapter 14—Defining Your Purpose*

In the chapter we reviewed four different types of people you have the opportunity to influence: family members, friends, workmates, and neighbors/strangers. As you think about the needs of the people in these four categories, what one goal can you set for yourself for this week to have an impact on...

Your family? One goal:

Your friends? One goal:

Your workmates? One goal:

Your neighbors/strangers? One goal:

Commit yourself to carrying out these goals this week!

What one truth from this chapter had the greatest impact on you, and why? Add this truth to your "One Truth List."

*Chapter 15—Practicing God's Plan*

In the previous chapter, we talked about goals for the physical, social, and vocational areas of your life. What improvements have you already noted?

Review the five key suggestions for handling your finances (see pages 151-52). In which two areas do you see the most room for improvement? What first steps can you take to make change happen?

With regard to setting goals for the family area of your life I wrote, "You and I need to do something every day to show our love. It doesn't have to be much. Little things go a long way." What "little things" have you done in the past that your wife has appreciated? Try to come up with one or two new ideas for "little things" you can do in the future.

With regard to setting goals for ministry: What is the purpose of your spiritual gifts, according to 1 Corinthians 12:7? What exhortation are we given in Hebrews 10:24-25?

What one truth from this chapter had the greatest impact on you, and why? Add this truth to your "One Truth List."

## Key #7—Purity

*Chapter 16—Dealing with Temptation*

Read again the section "Two Men, Two Choices, Two Paths." How do these two scenarios describe any of the struggles and paths you have faced in your life?

What encouragement can you draw from the four provisions God has supplied for you in dealing with temptation? Is there any one provision in particular you need to use today?

It *is* possible to resist temptation. Write 1 Corinthians 10:13 and Philippians 4:13 in the space below. Memorize one (or both!) of the verses so it stands ready to help encourage you whenever temptation strikes.

What one truth from this chapter had the greatest impact on you, and why? Remember to add this truth to your "One Truth List."

*Chapter 17—Fighting the Battle Against Temptation*
What are some of the "temptation battles" we face on a regular basis?

What are the four practical steps you can take to defend yourself against temptations of the flesh? (see pages 169-70).

What are some of the ways you can defend yourself against the temptations of worldliness?

What are the three suggested ways for defending against temptations of the devil?

When it comes to protecting yourself against temptation, are you proactive or reactive? That is, do you prepare yourself *before* temptation strikes, or do you let temptation catch you by surprise? What two or three things can you do to protect yourself *more* against temptation before it strikes?

What one truth from this chapter had the greatest impact on you, and why? Add this truth to your "One Truth List."

## Key #8—Service

*Chapter 18—Nurturing the Heart of a Servant*

Think of a Christian in your past who had a powerful impact on you through his service. What did that person do, and what effect did he have on you?

What can we learn from D.L. Moody's example of servanthood? (see pages 180-83).

The first insight on becoming a servant is to serve for a higher purpose. Because we serve with God and heaven in mind, earthly recognition and rewards shouldn't matter. What do you think is more important instead?

The second insight is to serve in spite of your situation. Are you allowing your current situation to keep you from serving God and His people? How does the advice from missionary T.J. Bach help you? (see page 183).

What one truth from this chapter had the greatest impact on you, and why? Add this truth to your "One Truth List."

### Chapter 19—Applying the Attitude of a Servant

The third insight on becoming a servant is to serve with integrity. What are some wrong motives for serving? What are some right motives?

The fourth insight is to serve to please God, and the fifth is to serve with pure motives. According to Galatians 1:10, is it possible to do our service to please both God and people? Why do you think that is the case?

The sixth insight is to serve with love. Read 1 Thessalonians 2:7-8. What qualities of Paul's service would you like to imitate more in your own life?

The seventh insight is to serve sacrificially. What are some examples of sacrifices we can make when serving family members? Fellow Christians? People in the workplace?

The eighth insight is to serve blamelessly. Why is this an important quality?

The ninth insight is to serve to nurture. Commit yourself to always building others up when you serve!

What one truth from this chapter had the greatest impact on you, and why? Add this truth to your "One Truth List."

## Key #9—Excellence

*Chapter 20—Cultivating Excellence*
What is the definition of excellence? (see page 196).

Look at the qualities that spell out E-X-C-E-L-L-E-N-C-E (see pages 199-203). In which two are you the strongest?

In which two are you the weakest?

What practical steps can you take—starting now—to improve in those two weak areas?

What one truth from this chapter had the greatest impact on you, and why? Remember to add this truth to your "One Truth List."

### Chapter 21—*Winning the Battle in the Secret Life*

Review the section "Your Secret Life and Excellence." Why is maintaining your inner life so important?

Part of nurturing your secret life is developing deep convictions. In what areas do you presently have strong convictions? Why are strong convictions helpful when it comes to living in an ungodly world?

A big part of having a healthy secret life is making right choices, especially in times of temptation. What can you do to help prepare yourself to make better choices when you find yourself tempted to do wrong?

List the four "determinations" that can deepen your commitment to excellence. Which one will you act on immediately, and how?

What one truth from this chapter had the greatest impact on you, and why? Add this truth to your "One Truth List."

## Key #10—Mentoring

*Chapter 22—Recognizing the Importance of Mentoring*
Think of a man who influenced your life positively in some way. What two or three key lessons did you learn from him?

Review the section about Paul's mentoring of others. What stands out to you about Paul's mentoring ministry?

Review the eight points of Jesus' mentoring process (see pages 221-23). Which one or two points stand out most to you, and why?

What are some key benefits of a mentoring relationship? And if you cannot find a one-on-one mentor, what are some other ways to get help and guidance?

What one truth from this chapter had the greatest impact on you, and why? Add this truth to your "One Truth List."

### Chapter 23—Leaving a Lasting Legacy

Take some time now to consider your influence on your wife, your children, your fellow Christians, and your world. What kind of impact are you having in these areas—is it an impact that brings honor to God? What must you do or change to ensure your influence will "live on" in a spiritual sense?

Are you a F-A-T man? (see page 230). Explain how you're doing in all three areas. Once again, are there changes you need to make?

What one truth from this chapter had the greatest impact on you, and why? Add this truth to your "One Truth List."

### Final Bonus Question

Review the "One Truth List" on pages 256-57. Which one has had the most impact on...

Your personal life?

Your home life?

Your public life?

Then take time to thank God that you are well on the road to becoming a man of influence, a man who leaves a lasting impact on others.

*Live on, my friend, live on!*

## One Truth List

List the truth in the chapter that had the greatest impact on you:

1. _____

2. _____

3. _____

4. _____

5. _____

6. _____

7. _____

8. _____

9. _____

10. _____

11. _____

12. _____

13. _____

14. _____

15. _____

16. _____

17. _____

18. _____

19. _____

20. _____

21. _____

22. _____

23. _____

# Notes

## Chapter 1—Profiling the Man Who Makes a Difference

1. Eleanor L. Doan, *The Speaker's Sourcebook* (Grand Rapids: Zondervan, 1977), p. 133.

2. John F. Kennedy, *Profiles in Courage,* inaugural edition (New York: Harper & Row, 1955).

3. John Pollock, *The Man Who Shook the World* (Wheaton, IL: Victor Books, 1973), p. 39.

4. Merrill C. Tenney, gen. ed., *The Zondervan Pictorial Encyclopedia of the Bible,* vol. 4 (Grand Rapids: Zondervan, 1975), p. 625.

5. D.A. Hayes, *Paul and His Epistles* (Grand Rapids: Baker, 1968).

6. Pollock, *The Man Who Shook the World.*

7. Source unknown.

## Chapter 2—Taking the First Step

1. As cited in *World Shapers* (Wheaton, IL: Harold Shaw, 1991), p. 16.

2. Doan, quoting Cal Stargel, "In This Day," *The Speaker's Sourcebook* (Grand Rapids: Zondervan, 1977), p. 133.

3. Charles R. Swindoll, *Paul: A Man of Grace and Grit* (Nashville, TN: W Publishing Group, 2002), p. 17.

4. Hymn "Hallelujah, What a Savior!" by Philip P. Bliss.

5. Author unknown, as cited in James Gilchrist Lawson, *The Best Loved Religious Poems* (New York: Fleming H. Revell, 1933), pp. 174-75.

## Chapter 3—Pursuing a Love for God's Word

1. Robert C. Chapman, *Choice Sayings* (London: Marshall, Morgan, & Scott, n.d.), p. 4.

**Chapter 4—Persevering for Life**

1. Howard G. Hendricks, *Living by the Book* (Chicago: Moody, 1991), p. 31.

**Chapter 5—Understanding the Significance of Prayer**

1. Jim George, *The Remarkable Prayers of the Bible* (Eugene, OR: Harvest House, 2005), p. 181.
2. Leonard Ravenhill, *Revival Praying* (Minneapolis: Bethany House, 1981).

**Chapter 6—Participating in a Life of Prayer**

1. E.M. Bounds, *The Complete Works of E.M. Bounds on Prayer* (Grand Rapids: Baker, 1990), p. 544.

**Chapter 7—Living a Life of Obedience**

1. Eric Liddell, as cited in *World Shapers* (Wheaton, IL: Harold Shaw, 1991), p. 90.

**Chapter 8—Following the Path of Obedience**

1. Hymn "Trust and Obey," written by John H. Sammis in 1887.

**Chapter 9—Mastering Life's Challenges**

1. Roy B. Zuck, *The Speaker's Quote Book* (Grand Rapids: Kregel, 1997), p. 16.
2. Romans 11:25; 1 Corinthians 12:1; 2 Corinthians 1:8; 1 Thessalonians 4:13 NKJV.
3. Zuck, *The Speaker's Quote Book,* p. 38.

**Chapter 10—Accepting the Challenge to Live Boldly**

1. John Witherspoon as cited in Albert M. Wells, Jr., *Inspiring Quotations—Contemporary and Classical* (Nashville, TN: Thomas Nelson, 1988), p. 73.

**Chapter 11—Pursuing Spiritual Discipline**

1. R. Kent Hughes, *Disciplines of a Godly Man* (Wheaton, IL: Crossway, 1991), p. 15.
2. John F. MacArthur, *The MacArthur New Testament Commentary—1 Timothy* (Chicago: Moody, 1995), p. 164.
3. Ibid.
4. Oswald Chambers as cited in Wells, *Inspiring Quotations,* p. 73.

## Chapter 12—Practicing Personal Discipline

1. Richard S. Taylor, *The Disciplined Life* (Minneapolis: Bethany House, 1962), p. 23.

2. V. Raymond Edman, *The Disciplines of Life* (Minneapolis: World Wide Publications, 1948), p. 9.

3. Taylor, *The Disciplined Life*, p. 23.

## Chapter 13—Developing Lifelong Goals

1. Edward R. Dayton and Ted W. Engstrom, *Strategy for Living* (Glendale, CA: Regal Books, 1978), p. 32.

## Chapter 14—Defining Your Purpose

1. A.B. Simpson as cited in Albert M. Wells, *Inspiring Quotations—Contemporary and Classical* (Nashville, TN: Thomas Nelson, 1988), p. 73.

2. Harry S. Truman as cited in Roy B. Zuck, *The Speaker's Quote Book* (Grand Rapids: Kregel, 1997), p. 344.

3. Kent Hughes, *Disciplines of a Godly Man* (Wheaton, IL: Crossway, 1991), pp. 62-63.

## Chapter 15—Practicing God's Plan

1. Henry R. Brandt as cited in Sherwood Eliot Wirt and Kersten Beckstrom, *Topical Encyclopedia of Living Quotations* (Minneapolis: Bethany House, 1982), p. 86.

## Chapter 16—Dealing with Temptation

1. Stephen Arterburn and Fred Stoeker, *Every Man's Battle* (Colorado Springs: WaterBrook, 2000), p. 4.

## Chapter 17—Fighting the Battle Against Temptation

1. Charles R. Swindoll, *The Quest for Character* (Portland, OR: Multnomah, 1987), p. 21.

2. Cited in Albert M. Wells, *Inspiring Quotations—Contemporary and Classical* (Nashville, TN: Thomas Nelson, 1988), p. 128.

3. Pushon, as cited in D.L. Moody, *Notes from My Bible and Thoughts from My Library* (Grand Rapids, MI: Baker, 1979), p. 331.

**Chapter 18—Nurturing the Heart of a Servant**

1. Douglas Groothuis as cited in *Checklist for Life for Men* (Nashville, TN: Thomas Nelson, 2002), p. 135.

2. John Whiteley as cited in *World Shapers* (Wheaton, IL: Harold Shaw, 1991), p. 121.

3. T.J. Bach as cited in *World Shapers,* p. 75.

**Chapter 19—Applying the Attitude of a Servant**

1. John C. Maxwell, *The 21 Indispensable Qualities of a Leader* (Nashville, TN: Thomas Nelson, 1999), pp. 135-36.

2. Jim George, *God's Wisdom for Little Boys* (Eugene, OR: Harvest House, 2002).

**Chapter 20—Cultivating Excellence**

1. Gary Inrig, *A Call to Excellence* (Wheaton, IL: Victor Books, 1985).

2. Inrig, *A Call to Excellence,* p. 87.

3. Sid Buzzell, gen. ed., *The Leadership Bible* (Grand Rapids: Zondervan, 1998), p. 1366.

**Chapter 21—Winning the Battle in the Secret Life**

1. John C. Maxwell, *The 21 Indispensable Qualities of a Leader* (Nashville, TN: Thomas Nelson, 1999), p. 20.

**Chapter 22—Recognizing the Importance of Mentoring**

1. Warren Webster as cited in Charles R. Swindoll, *The Tale of the Tardy Oxcart* (Nashville, TN: Word, 1998), p. 300.

2. Robert E. Coleman, *The Master Plan of Evangelism* (Old Tappan, NJ: Revell, 1987), p. 7.

## An Invitation to Write

Jim George is a teacher and speaker and the author of *A Man After God's Own Heart*. If you would like to receive more information about other books and audiotapes by Jim George, or if you want to share how *The Man Who Makes a Difference* has influenced your life, you can write to him at:

Jim George
P.O. Box 2879
Belfair, WA 98528
Toll-free fax/phone: 1-800-542-4611
www.JimGeorge.com

### THE BARE BONES BIBLE® HANDBOOK

The perfect resource for a fast and friendly overview of every book of the Bible. Excellent for knowing more about the Bible and getting more from your interaction with God's Word.

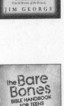

### THE BARE BONES BIBLE® HANDBOOK FOR TEENS

The Bible is a big book filled with lots of information. How can you ever get to know it and use it in your everyday life? This resource looks at the big idea of each book of the Bible, the main events, and the important lessons for personal and spiritual growth.

### THE BARE BONES BIBLE® BIOS

Meet the remarkable men and women of Scripture—through David, Esther, Paul, Mary, and others who lived centuries ago, you can learn powerfully relevant lessons for today.

### THE BARE BONES BIBLE® FACTS

A concise and friendly A-to-Z survey of the people, places, and things of the Bible, with life lessons from key Bible characters, practical applications for everyday living, and charts and maps that enhance clarity and understanding.

### A Husband After God's Own Heart

You will find your marriage growing richer and deeper as you pursue God and discover 12 areas in which you can make a real difference in your relationship with your wife.

### A Man After God's Own Heart

This book explores God's perfect design for you in all the key areas of your life—your marriage, children, work, church, and life witness to others. You'll come to know the satisfaction of living a life of biblical purpose.

### A Young Man After God's Own Heart

Pursuing God really is an adventure—a lot like climbing up a mountain. There are all kinds of challenges on the way up, but the awesome view at the top is well worth the trip. This book will help you to experience the thrill of knowing real success in life—the kind that counts with God.

### The Remarkable Prayers of the Bible

Discover practical lessons in the thought-provoking prayers of Nehemiah, Moses, Abraham, and many others—well over a hundred exciting and useful applications that will help you take strides toward growth and maturity.

### God Loves His Precious Children
*(coauthored with Elizabeth George)*

Jim and Elizabeth George share the comfort and assurance of Psalm 23 with younger children. Engaging watercolor scenes by artist Judy Luenebrink and delightful rhymes by Jim and Elizabeth bring the truths of each verse to life.

### God's Wisdom for Little Boys
*(coauthored with Elizabeth George)*

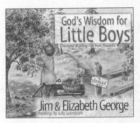

The wonderful teachings of Proverbs come to life for boys. Memorable rhymes play alongside colorful paintings for a charming presentation of truths to live by.

### A Little Boy After God's Own Heart
*(coauthored with Elizabeth George)*

The combination of charming paintings and easy-to-learn lessons will guide boys toward the heart of God and toward a life of godliness that shows in their words, actions, and spirit.